GRIM
AND CO

GRIM CRIMS
AND CONVICTS

1788 – 1820

Jackie French

Illustrations and cartoons by
Peter Sheehan

A Scholastic Press book
from Scholastic Australia

Scholastic Press
345 Pacific Highway
Lindfield NSW 2070
an imprint of Scholastic Australia Pty Limited (ABN 11 000 614 577)
PO Box 579
Gosford NSW 2250
www.scholastic.com.au

Part of the Scholastic Group
Sydney • Auckland • New York • Toronto • London • Mexico City
• New Delhi • Hong Kong • Buenos Aires • Puerto Rico

First published by Scholastic Press in 2005.
This edition published in 2009.
Text copyright © Jackie French, 2005.
Illustrations and cartoons copyright © Clop Pty Ltd, 2005.
Illustrations and cartoons by Peter Sheehan.
Internal design and typesetting by Lloyd Foye & Associates.
Editorial consultant, Kate McAllan.

National Library of Australia Cataloguing-in-Publication entry

French, Jackie.
Grim crims & convicts.

For upper primary/lower secondary students.
ISBN 978-1-74169-314-0
1. Australia - History - To 1788 - Juvenile fiction.
2. Australia - History - 1788-1851 - Juvenile fiction.
I. Sheehan, Peter, 1964- . II. Title. (Series : Fair dinkum
histories).

A823.3

Typeset in 11.5/15pt Espirit Book

Printed by McPherson's Printing Group, Victoria.

10 9 8 7 6 5 4 3   10 11 12 13 14 15 / 0

CONTENTS

VERY MESSY HISTORY

It's difficult to know exactly what happened back in the early days of the colony. The only way we can find out is if someone wrote about it in their diaries or letters or reports. But often four people would write about the same event—and they would all say different things. So who do we believe?

Sometimes people were reporting what someone else had told them; sometimes people tried to turn an event into a more interesting story for people back home in England to read. And none of them probably had any idea that, hundreds of years later, we would be reading their words, trying to work out exactly what happened when! For this reason, some of the things you'll read in *Grim Crims & Convicts* may be different from what you'll find in other books.

And remember, there are always two sides to a story!

CHAPTER 1

A SPOT ON THE BOTTOM OF THE WORLD

It was an incredible idea—to found a colony of convicts eight months' sail away from Great Britain. In a land with no cities, no farms, no rich spices, just 'savages' in huts.

The Dutch, the French and the Portuguese had known about the land down-under for two hundred years—and had turned their noses up at it. The Chinese had known about it for even longer, and they weren't interested either.

The colonists would have to take everything with them in their tiny ships: from needles to flour, spades, seeds, boots, medicine, fruit trees and even chamber pots. Enough to last them for years.

No country had ever thought to send colonists so far away. Why on earth would you bother?

A Foothold Down-Under

New Holland, as it was then known, just happened to be in the right place at the right time.

Britain had been at war with France and Holland, and British ships hadn't been able to call in at the Dutch ports in South Africa to restock with food and water on their way to India, China, Korea, Japan and north-west America.

It looked like war might be coming again. The British needed a base in the southern hemisphere—fast!

So they decided to found a colony.

Round and Round in Circles

The first choice was up the River Gambia, in West Africa. But people were outraged! British settlers would die of disease if they were sent to this hot, harsh place!

So another place was chosen ... the region around Das Voltas Bay in South Africa. But a scouting party reported that this site was just a barren rocky shore.

Then came the news that the French were sending garrisons to the East Indies. They might even attack the British settlements in India. Things were getting urgent! Should the new colony be on Norfolk Island, with its flax plants and pines? Or New Zealand?

Finally Sir Joseph Banks, who had sailed with Captain Cook, convinced the government that Botany Bay in New Holland was the best place in the world for a new colony.

BANKING ON BOTANY BAY

According to Banks, Botany Bay was perfect. The soil was fertile. The big trees were ideal for building ships and houses. There were plenty of fish, said Banks, and there was lush grass that cattle would thrive on, and there were no dangerous wild beasts. Maybe spices could even be grown there. The pines of nearby Norfolk Island would provide masts for the Royal Navy, and New Zealand's flax plants would provide canvas sails and cordage for the Royal Navy.

And Botany Bay was already British. Captain Cook had claimed the coast of New Holland in 1770—although no-one had yet told this to the people who actually lived there. But the original inhabitants were very few, said Banks, and they were armed only with spears tipped with fish bones.

There was just one problem. Botany Bay was too far away for anyone to go and take a second look. But surely Sir Joseph Banks must have got it right...

Actually, Banks was wrong about almost everything. And by the time the colonists found out, it was too late!

SELECTING THE SETTLERS

Few people would be rash enough to sail around the world to an unknown land. Not even when the great Sir Joseph Banks said it was a fine place. But the British Government had a good stock of people who would go wherever they were told. And they would work for nothing when they got there. Convicts!

WHAT DO WE DO WITH THE CRIMS?

Convicts used to be sent to the American colonies. Then, in 1775, those colonies seized independence and declared war on Britain. The British thought that the war would soon be over. So while the British were waiting to win, the convicts were kept in 'hulks' moored in the busy rivers and harbours of southern England.

But the war took eight years—and the American colonies won!

So what should be done with the convicts?

The cheapest solution was to keep them working in England. But in a new colony, the convicts might have a chance to make a new life for themselves too. And maybe the threat of being sent so far away would make the criminals at home behave themselves.

WHAT ABOUT THE LOCALS?

The British Government asked Sir Joseph Banks if the local people of New Holland would sell the British some land. Banks replied that the locals were only interested in food. He believed they would abandon the country when the new colonists arrived.

He was wrong about this too.

A MOTLEY CREW OF SETTLERS

Australia's first white settlers were mostly unwilling, lazy, dirty—and criminals. Nearly all the convicts were thieves—pickpockets, sheep stealers, poachers. There were also seven swindlers and four forgers, but no murderers or rapists. Most were young—but not healthy: they were starved and ragged from the filthy, disease-wracked prisons and hulks.

According to some records, the 'First Fleet' of eleven ships carried 1467 people. These included:

759 convicts
13 convicts' kids
252 marines, including
   their wives and children
210 Royal Navy seamen
233 merchant seamen

Merchant seamen were sailors hired by the British admiralty to take the convicts to New Holland.

The seamen would not stay in the colony, but would sail the ships back to England.

HANGIN'S TOO GOOD FOR 'EM

Many First Fleeters had been convicted of stealing small things like a handkerchief, a cheese, a packet of snuff, twelve cucumber plants or a book.

But most had actually stolen much more.

In those days, if you stole goods worth more than forty shillings from a house, or five shillings from a shop, you had to be hanged. But if the judge thought you had a chance to reform, he would decide to find you guilty of stealing only two or three of the things you'd actually stolen, and send you to join the navy. Or else transport you to a new land.

> In dirty London with its poverty and crime, experienced criminals would gather 'schools' of young kids and train them to become pickpockets and thieves.

Prison sentences were for seven years, fourteen years or for life. 'Lifers' and 'fourteen-year chums' were the ones most likely to be transported, but jailers found many others to fill up the numbers in the ships—especially people who had been unruly in prison or in the hulks.

POOR MAN, BEGGAR MAN, THIEF

Eleven percent of the men in the First Fleet had once been farm labourers. There were also two gardeners and two fishermen, ten cobblers, six carpenters, fourteen weavers, two bricklayers, two jewellers, two bakers and a scattering of other trades. Most of the women had been servants, as well as oyster sellers and cloak, hat and glove makers.

What's worse? What you do, or getting caught doing it?

Even though these people had a trade, they may not have had jobs. Once the wars with America and France were over, many soldiers and sailors were unemployed too. There was no unemployment benefit. If you didn't have a job you starved—or stole. But there were also many professional thieves, who never thought of being anything else.

THE YOUNGEST CONVICT BOY

John Hudson was thirteen years old when he sailed on the the First Fleet. There were younger children on board, but they were the children of convict women or of marines and were not convicts themselves.

John was an orphan, a chimneysweep and a thief. His life had been hell . . .

Children as young as four were sold to masters and made to climb up inside chimneys to scrape away the soot. Sooty chimneys often caught fire, and kids were sent into the still-burning chimneys to put the fires out.

Chimneysweeps needed to be small to fit into the small spaces. They were starved so they wouldn't grow too big. Their legs and backs grew twisted from climbing and they were forbidden to wash in case it softened their skin. Their skin was covered in sores that often turned into cancers. If they got stuck in a chimney, the masters tied ropes around their arms or legs to haul them out, even though this sometimes broke the chimneysweeps' backs.

Few chimneysweeps lived to adulthood. It would be hard to blame starved little John Hudson for stealing.

John was charged with breaking and entering and burglary. But a kind judge decided to convict him only for breaking and entering. If he'd been convicted of the burglary as well, he'd have been hanged. John was sentenced to seven years transportation. He was only nine years old.

John stayed on the hulks for years before the First Fleet sailed. He then survived the eight-month journey into the unknown.

What Happened Then?

We know John was sent to Norfolk Island in 1790. We know that Major Ross ordered he be given fifty lashes for being outside his hut after-hours.

But after that, little John Hudson is never mentioned again. Perhaps he eventually went to Van Diemen's Land with the rest of the convicts from Norfolk Island. Maybe he lived a long and prosperous life, was given a ticket-of-leave and a grant of land and established a family. Or maybe the youngest convict boy rests without a gravestone, somewhere on Norfolk Island.

Governor
Arthur
Phillip

Chapter 2

Fitting Out the Fleet

The British Government wasn't too sure what Botany Bay was like. It didn't know how long it would take to get there, or even how long it would take to sail between Botany Bay and the Cape of Good Hope in South Africa for supplies.

Follow the Leader

Captain Arthur Phillip was semiretired. That is, he was a naval captain getting half pay, and living as a farmer, waiting until the navy might need him again. He had already retired once, when he was twenty-five, to become a farmer and get married. But the marriage failed and farming bored him, so after seven years he had joined the navy again.

Phillip had never done anything like lead a new colony. But now he was going to leave his farm again, this time to take more than a thousand people to the far side of the world and set up a colony there.

Phillip dreamed of founding a new part of the British Empire. It would be a land where each man would grow his own food, where convicts would be kept separately from free settlers, even once they were free, and where there would never be slavery.

It was a grand dream. But would it work?

CROOKED CONTRACTORS

The colony almost failed before it began. Ignorant government officials tried to supply the fleet with only enough food to get to the Bahamas. They provided no cloth for new clothes, and only six scythes for the entire colony.

But Phillip pleaded and demanded. He wanted his fleet to be the best equipped—and the healthiest—that Britain had ever known. And when the fleet reached its destination, he wanted the colony to have enough tools to survive.

The Ships of the First Fleet

There were eleven ships in the First Fleet. HMS *Sirius* and *Supply* were Royal Navy ships, carrying naval men and officers. The *Alexander*, *Charlotte*, *Friendship*, *Scarborough*, *Prince of Wales* and *Lady Penrhyn* were merchant ships, hired specially to transport the convicts. And there were three storeships—*Borrowdale*, *Golden Grove* and *Fishburn*. The ships were all small—the largest was only thirty-six metres long—and very, very crowded!

All Aboard!

The First Fleet ships were moored in Plymouth Harbour, about 250 kilometres south-west of London. Most of the prisoners, however, were in London prisons, or hulks on the Thames. So the prisoners were chained and sent to Plymouth in open carts, then marched to the quay and rowed in small boats out to the waiting ships.

As soon as they were on board their filthy rags were stripped off. They were washed in two big tubs of water—not to get them clean, but to get rid of fleas and lice.

The convicts were then given coarse, off-white shirts and trousers (the convict arrows came later). Their chains were put back on, they climbed down the ladder into the space below the deck, and then the ladder was hauled up to stop them escaping.

It was dark down there, and it stank. There were no candles or lamps (in case of fire); no portholes; and no fresh air unless the hatch was open—but in bad weather, or while the ship was in port, the hatch was kept shut.

Once a disease caught hold on a ship it could spread to everyone on board. Some ships were found floating and empty on the open sea, everyone dead of plague or typhus, or with too few surviving crew members to sail to port.

For a while the prisoners were taken ashore in chains every day to work in work-gangs. But in the few weeks just before they sailed they just sat and waited.

Those who could write sent letters to their loved ones— letters of despair and longing. Would they ever see England again? The convicts might be free in seven or fourteen years, but could they ever afford the fare back? Would they even survive the voyage? It was common for one third of all sailors to die on a bad voyage—even if they weren't shipwrecked. There were no radios

or phones to call for help if a ship got into trouble. Most ships only carried one or two lifeboats, which wasn't enough to save everybody. Few people, if any, could swim. And no-one can swim in chains.

What would the land be like when they arrived? Would they starve? Would there be monsters? Cannibals?

KIDS ON THE FIRST FLEET

There were about thirty-four children under the age of fourteen aboard the First Fleet when it sailed. Another twenty babies were born on the voyage, though some of them died. About fifty kids went ashore when the fleet reached Port Jackson.

ELIZABETH HAYWARD

Elizabeth was about thirteen when the First Fleet sailed—the youngest of the women convicts. She had stolen a linen gown and a silk bonnet worth seven shillings from the man she was apprenticed to. She was sentenced to seven years' transportation and sent out on the *Lady Penrhyn*. According to Captain Phillip's letters, most of the women had arrived on the ship filthy and almost naked. Many were ill from prison fevers.

As on the other ships, conditions on board the *Lady Penrhyn* were as good as Phillip was able to make them—but even so they were dark, cramped and stinking. Many of the women had dreadful seasickness. They also suffered injuries from falls and from being thrown from their berths during storms.

When the ship arrived at Port Jackson, Elizabeth was assigned to the Reverend Richard Johnson as a servant. Not long after, she was given thirty lashes of the whip for insolence. She was fifteen, and would have carried the scars all her life.

Elizabeth was sent to Norfolk Island in 1790, and was probably freed there when she had served out her sentence. She married on the island and was one of the last colonists to leave for Van Diemen's Land, along with her husband Joseph Lowe and her two children.

An Elizabeth Lowe was buried in Launceston in 1836, aged sixty-six. This is possibly the same Elizabeth who sailed on the First Fleet. Maybe the convict girl had a happy and fulfilling life as a farmer and mother after her harsh early years.

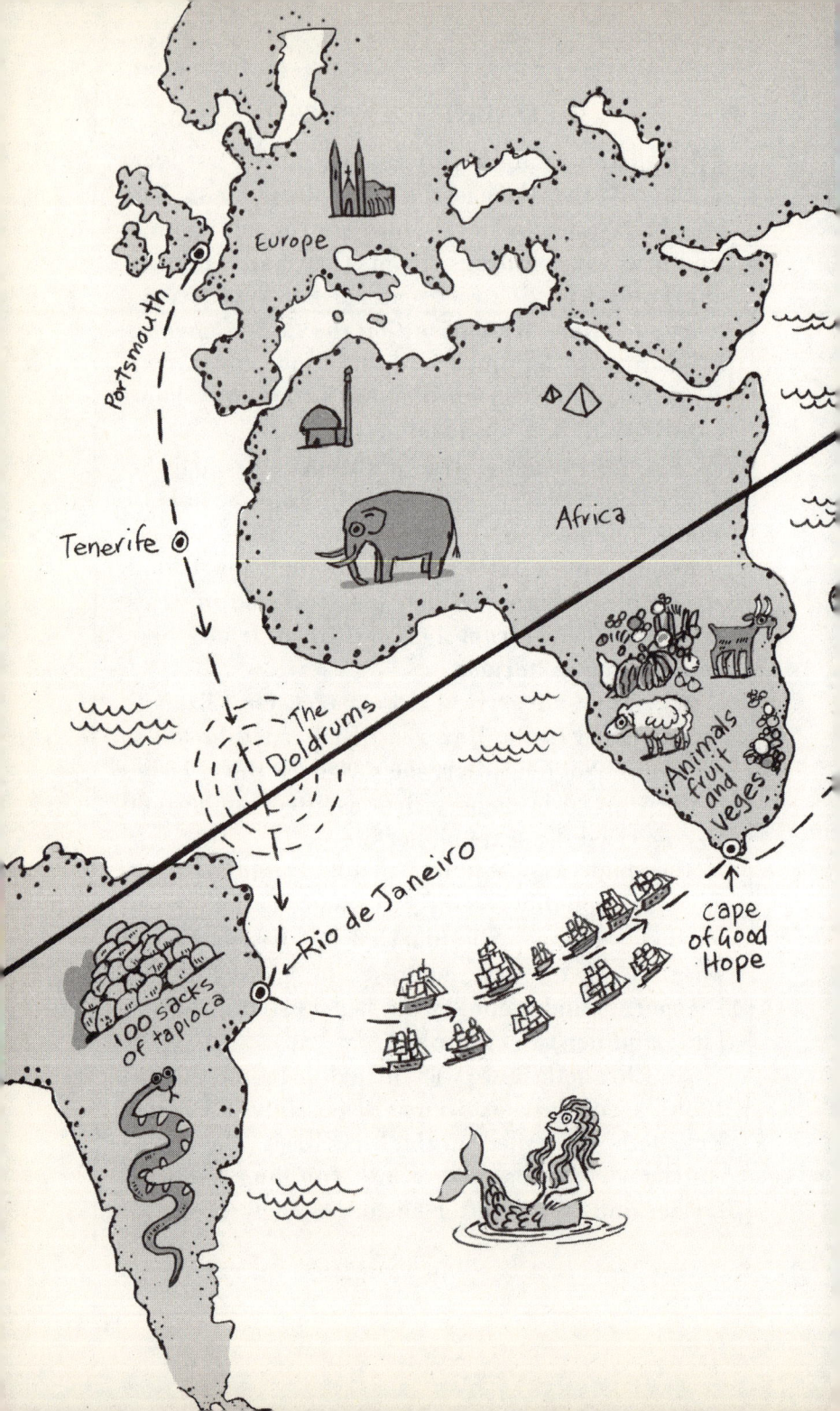

Equator

Botany Bay →

Trade Winds

Storms

Chapter 3
Bound for Botany Bay

The First Fleet sailed in May 1787.

By modern standards, the journey from England to New Holland was hell—stinking, terrifying, crowded, with rotting food to eat and stale water to drink. But by eighteenth-century standards, it was a miracle voyage. In the course of the eight-month journey, only thirty-one of Phillip's charges died. Those deaths were from childbirth, or else from illnesses people already had when they came aboard. This was far fewer than would have died if they had stayed in prison in England, or even in the slums of London. Once the ships left England, there were no major outbreaks of disease.

This miracle was due to Captain Arthur Phillip's determination and excellent planning.

Poo, Stink and Spew

Below deck it was dark: the only light came from the hatch. There were no toilets, just buckets that were emptied (but not washed) once a day. In rough weather they weren't emptied at all—but that didn't matter, because in rough weather the buckets tipped over, and no-one could stand (or sit) to use them anyway. The floor was constantly awash with filthy water, dead rats and all the muck that hadn't made it to the toilet buckets.

The foul holds stank in the hot weather. The smell from the convicts was so bad that it even made the marines guarding the hatches feel faint.

There were two rows of sleeping berths, a bit like double bunks. Each one was less than two square metres, about the size of a double bed, and three convicts shared each berth. There were no mattresses, no pillows, and just one blanket each. And there was nothing to stop people rolling off.

Most days the convicts were allowed up on deck, still chained to prevent them taking over the ship. But when the ship was in port, or in bad weather, the convicts had to stay below. The weather was often bad—and there were never enough buckets for seasickness!

WHAT'S FOR DINNER?

Convicts were fed twice a day—but only if the weather wasn't too rough for the buckets of food to be lowered down to them. Their food was mostly soup or stew, with hard bread or ship's biscuit. The convicts filled their pannikins from the food buckets. If they were weak or sick they missed out, unless a friend collected their rations for them.

Due to crooked contractors, the convicts were often given weevilly rice instead of bread.

The rations for each adult man for a week were:

3 kg salt beef *or*

1.8 kg salt pork, *stewed with*

1.7 L dried peas, *plus*

500 g flour (about 2 thick slices of bread a day)

200 g salty, rancid butter

Women received two thirds of this.

But when the ships called in at Tenerife, Rio de Janeiro and Cape Town, Phillip ordered that the convicts eat all the fresh fruit they could, as well as fresh meat and vegetables, to help prevent scurvy during the next leg of the voyage.

The Dogleg Route

The ships sailed from Portsmouth to Tenerife; then across the Atlantic to Rio de Janeiro in Brazil; then back across the Atlantic to the Cape of Good Hope in South Africa. On a map, this looks like the long way around, but by following this route the fleet caught the best winds and was also aided by the current from Brazil.

In the days before engines, ships needed good winds and currents to move them along. Near the equator, there are places where there is very little wind at all. These are the *doldrums*. Whole crews have starved or died of thirst on ships caught in the windless doldrums.

Calling In for Takeaways

The fleet called in at three ports for fresh food and water. At Rio de Janeiro, Phillip bought a hundred sacks of tapioca so that the women could make clothes for themselves out of the tough bags.

It stayed a month in Cape Town to buy seeds, plants and animals for the new colony. Two bulls, three cows and seven horses were brought on board along with hens, pigs, sheep and goats. Many officers and marines bought animals, trees and seeds for themselves, too, and everything was crammed in below. This made the crowding—and the smell—even worse. For that whole month the convicts had to stay below decks, sweltering in the stink, in case they tried to escape.

THE OCEAN OF STORMS

The most terrifying part of the voyage was yet to come: the emptiness of the Indian Ocean, the unknown seas and lands beyond—not to mention the dreadful swells off the Cape of Good Hope. These were ship destroyers—giant waves where the Atlantic and Indian Oceans met. They towered above the fleet so that each ship had to climb a hill of water, then crash back down the other side.

Even after the Cape, the storms continued—though at least the winds helped sweep the ships on their way. Further

OFFICERS' ITCH
At sea, clothes could only be washed in salt water. This turned clothes stiff and made them itchy. Sailors and convicts wore loose trousers that didn't rub them raw; women convicts wore skirts (and no underpants). But officers wore close-fitting trousers which became desperately uncomfortable after a time at sea.

storms crashed about the fleet as it sailed south of New Holland. Lightning and wind split the *Golden Grove*'s topsail and blew the *Prince of Wales*' mainyard away. It was too rough to let the convicts up on deck. They had to stay below, clinging to their bunks.

CHAPTER 4

LAND HO!

The ships sailed south of Van Diemen's Land, and then up the east coast of the continent of New Holland without ever seeing land. But Phillip and his sailors knew it was there— they could tell from the birds and the shape of the waves.

Phillip had divided the fleet in two after they left the Cape, so that the fastest ships could go ahead and get to Botany Bay first.

Finally, on 3 January 1788, after eight long months of hardship and hunger, the lookout on the *Supply* saw land for the first time since leaving the Cape. But the ships were driven back south again by the current and strong winds. Then, on 18 January, *Supply* made it into Botany Bay. By 20 January the whole fleet had arrived. They were safe!

Or were they? Was this really the good land that Sir Joseph Banks had promised? Or had he fluffed it?

Strangers on Strange Ships

What did the First Fleet look like to the watchers on the shore—the Cadigal people of the Eora? The Cadigal had seen giant ships with flapping sails before. But in 1770, Captain Cook's ships had sailed away again, leaving nothing but a few stories to tell around the fire.

This time there were more ships. Even so, there was no reason for the Cadigal to think they meant to stay. And even if they did stay, the newcomers were outnumbered. And those pale-faced, sick-looking people on the ships didn't even seem to have spears or throwing sticks . . .

The First Spear Is Thrown

Phillip ordered several parties to go ashore to cut grass for the animals, find fresh water, and scout the land. But as more and more people began to disembark from the ships, the watchers on the shore grew wary.

The First White Bum on the Beach

Every time the newcomers raised their hats the Cadigal gave a roar of delight. They were incredibly curious about the newcomers. Why did they wear those strange garments in the heat of summer? There was an even greater mystery: were these weird people men or women? The newcomers all had hairless faces, but their really interesting bits were hidden under bulky—and by now very smelly—clothes.

Finally Lieutenant King ordered one of his men to open his trousers to settle the matter—which brought more roars of enjoyment from the Cadigal.

Culture Clash

The Eora and the British were as different as two groups of people could be. They were so different that they almost never understood each other.

The British were led by kings and queens who got their power through inheritance. The Eora were led by elders—wise, usually elderly, men and women who passed on their knowledge only to those who were steady and intelligent.

The British had schools and wrote their knowledge down, whereas the Eora learnt from life and passed their knowledge from person to person.

The British divided days into hours, minutes and seconds. The Eora had no words for these, but they had words for more seasons than the British had dreamt of.

The British had traded knowledge with many lands for centuries. The people of Australia had lived in almost complete isolation for thousands of years.

The British paid for goods with money. The Eora gave gifts as a way of cementing friendship.

The British believed that food belonged to the person who had hunted it, fished it, bought it or grown it—and that anyone taking that food was stealing. The Eora shared all food.

The British divided land into farms that people owned. The Eora didn't own land, they belonged to it.

THE EORA

People who speak the same language in an area are called a *language group*. In 1788 there were over five hundred languages spoken in Australia. *Eora* was the name given to the people in the area we now know as Sydney. *Eora* simply meant *here* or *from this place*. The Eora were part of the bigger Dharuk language group.

THE PEOPLE OF THE SYDNEY AREA

DHARUK (Darug): included the Eora and country from the mouth of the Hawkesbury River at Broken Bay, along the Hawkesbury and Nepean Rivers as far south as Camden.

DHARAWAL (Tharawal): south of Botany Bay (Thirroul is named after the Dharawal); all of modern-day Sutherland Shire; and down past Wollongong.

GURINGAI: north of Port Jackson and surrounding Broken Bay.

The language groups were divided into bands or family groups. For instance, the Cadigal, who lived around Sydney Cove, were part of the Dharuk language group. However, most of the Aboriginal people of the Port Jackson area were killed by warfare or disease before their cultures were properly recorded.

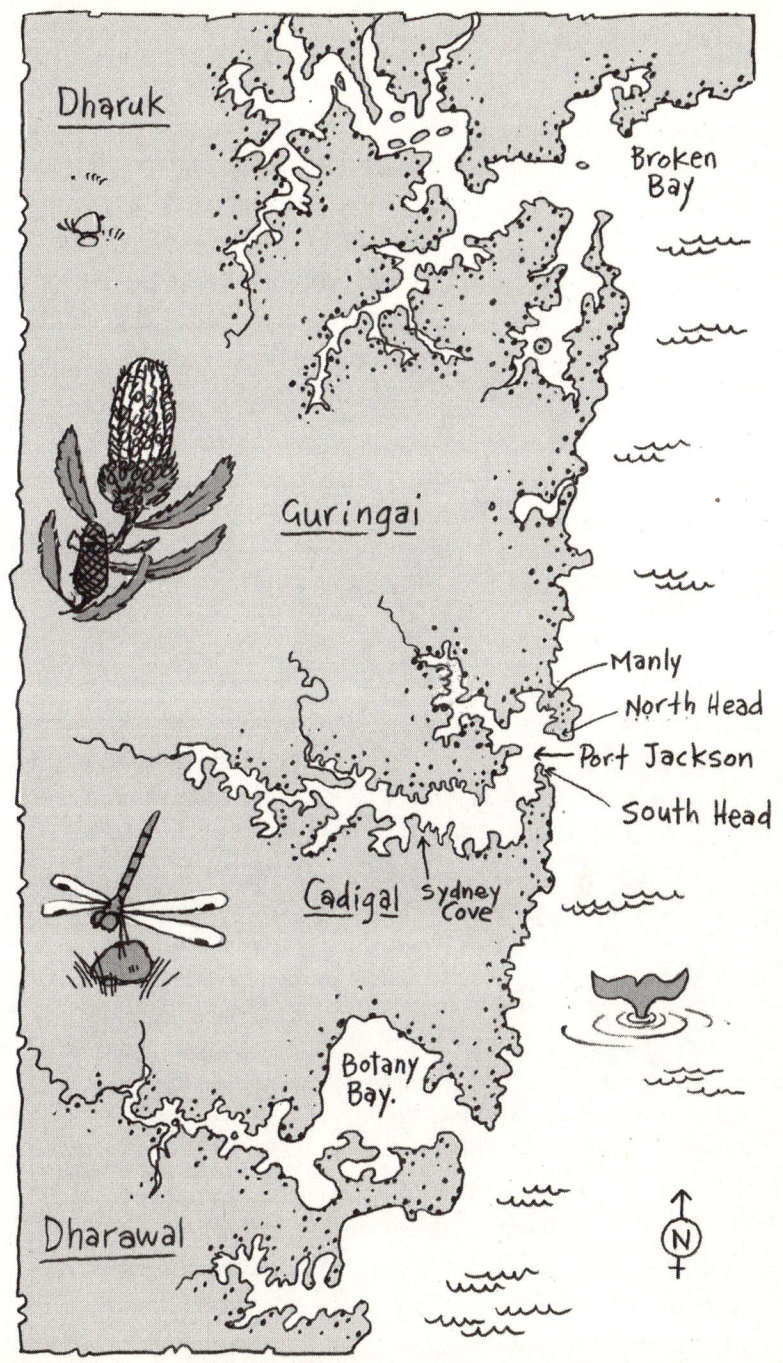

Dharuk

Broken Bay

Guringai

Manly
North Head
Port Jackson
South Head

Cadigal
Sydney Cove

Botany Bay.

Dharawal

N

Two Worlds Collide

Some of the British were fascinated by Eora culture, and wanted to learn more. Others wanted to live in peace with the Eora, although they thought that the Eora should live like the British and wear clothes, live in houses and work for money.

But most of Australia's early white settlers were criminals, ignorant and bigoted. For convicts at the bottom of the social system, it felt good to find someone they could pretend were even lower than themselves.

The British could never understand why the Eora people accepted gifts of beads or bits of cloth—then threw them away! But the Eora used presents like we use Christmas cards: they're not worth much, and they get thrown away after Christmas, but they're a way of saying 'Hey, you're my friend'.

As for the free settlers, they were battling a climate they didn't understand. They were also battling loneliness and the challenge of clearing land and building shelter. The Eora were just another threat in a threatening land.

Sir Joseph Banks

BANKS BLEW IT

There were a lot more Aboriginal people than Banks had said there would be. But he had made worse mistakes than that. For this was not the rich land that Banks had promised. The Aboriginal people lived in comfort, but the British soon realised that they themselves might all be dead within a year.

The lush-looking grass was long and coarse. The big trees Banks had praised were hollow or twisted and only good for firewood. The so-called 'rich soil' was nothing but black sand. Even the sheltered harbour they had expected could only be reached by passing over a dangerous sandbar. But there was no turning back.

WE'RE OUTTA HERE!

The new colony needed fresh water, good soil, and a safe place for their ships. But did such a place exist? Captain Cook had already mapped the coast, and he and Banks had said that Botany Bay was the best spot. Was it really? Had the First Fleet come so far only to be doomed? Phillip could only hope that there was somewhere better that Cook had missed. So he and a search party sailed up the coast to check out Port Jackson.

What a Bewdy!

The colonists needed a miracle—and they got it. On 24 January 1788 the search party came back with grins like slices of watermelon. Only a few hours' sail north of Botany Bay they had found one of the finest harbours in the world. It could hold one thousand ships! It had deep coves where large ships could anchor close to shore, and the heads were close enough together to defend the land against enemy ships as well. The new harbour also had better soil than Botany Bay, as well as fresh water.

> How had Cook missed it? The winds had been too strong for Cook to sail through the heads, but he did notice that there was some sort of bay beyond the rocky headlands.

The colony had a chance to survive!

Strewth!

One of the main reasons for coming to Botany Bay was to keep the French away from New Holland. But just as the fleet was about to sail for Port Jackson, two strange ships sailed into Botany Bay. Were they Dutch ships, about to throw out

the English settlers? (After all, Holland had also claimed New Holland.) Or were they storeships from England?

They were in fact French ships, the *Boussole* and the *Astrolabe*, under the command of the Comte de La Pérouse. For the time being, France and England were not at war and these two ships were just on a scientific expedition. Even so, their arrival proved that the English had claimed their South Pacific base just in time!

Good harbours and deep rivers were vitally important. Ships couldn't anchor safely unless they were protected from storms— and without ships you couldn't trade or travel.

A CLOSE SHAVE

The First Fleet had sailed safely across the world. But as they headed out of Botany Bay they ran into a fierce headwind, and two ships ran into each other. Then a third ship crashed into them! The other ships milled around, trying to stay clear of each other and the rocks. Fortunately, the damaged ships were still able to sail, and the First Fleet finally left the bay, leaving the French ships behind.

Thomas Townshend,
'Lord Sydney'

CHAPTER 5

OFF TO A SHAKY START

No-one watching the arrival of the First Fleet could have believed that this ragged, smelly mob of convicts and marines would be the foundations of a future nation.

FOR KING AND COUNTRY

On the evening of 25 January 1788 Captain Phillip, on board the *Supply*, sailed into Port Jackson. The ship dropped anchor in a bay and Captain Phillip named it Sydney Cove, after the bloke who had sent them all that way: Lord Sydney. But no-one landed that night.

Early next morning, Phillip and some of his officers and a few convicts went ashore. Phillip ordered that trees be cleared away from the banks of a freshwater stream—the Tank Stream. He also ordered that a flagpole be put up. Then Phillip claimed possession of the land in the name of King George III and the British flag was raised.

A few hours later the remaining ten ships sailed into Port Jackson, their sails full, the sailors and marines crowding the decks to look at the place that would be their home. What did those first settlers see? A harbour more glorious than any they had known; green forest growing right down to the rocks that edged the harbour; smoke from Eora cooking fires dusting up between the trees; and canoes so low in the water that the women in them seemed almost to be sitting in the water.

> Eora women fished with nets or lines, and grilled fish for their children in tiny, almost smokeless, fires in their canoes.

It was beautiful. It was strange. And it was probably far less terrifying than the dangers the newcomers had faced so far.

LAYING A CLAIM

The only places Phillip was told to occupy were Botany Bay and Norfolk Island. However, he was ordered to claim a third of the continent of New Holland, from Cape York to South Cape, as well as inland to 135° east. Phillip also claimed the 'adjacent islands' for Britain—which meant he claimed New Zealand and Tahiti.

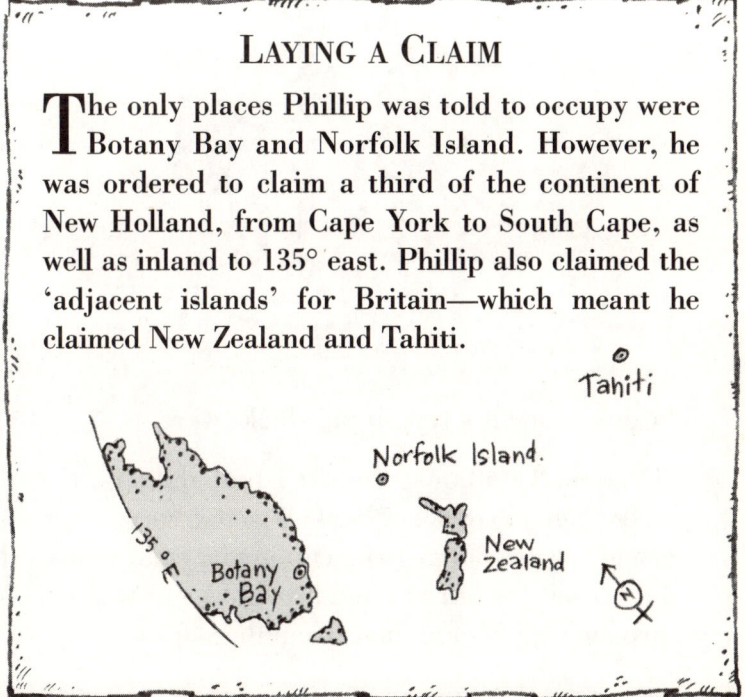

Out on the harbour, most of the convicts still huddled in the stink below deck, sweating in the heat, locked away in case they took over the ships and tried to sail back to England.

GETTING SETTLED

By the second evening there were tents amongst the trees, and fancy marquees for the officers. A blacksmith's forge was set up, and stones gathered for cooking fires. On 29 January a canvas house was erected for Governor Phillip.

NO NOAH'S ARK

On the third day the animals were brought ashore. Many had died on the way from Cape Town, either from injuries or starvation.

Why the long face?

The government's remaining stocks were:

4 mares; 2 stallions; 4 cows; 1 bull and a bull calf; 'a good stock' of hens; 3 goats; hogs; 'some' ewes (there is no mention of a ram, so it's lucky that the officers had brought their own private supply of animals from the Cape!).

There was almost no clear land, so trees had to be felled. As more land was cleared, more male convicts came ashore, though the women and children still stayed on the ships.

Phillip realised that many of the convicts were sick with scurvy. They needed fresh vegetables, so a garden was immediately started next to the tent hospital.

Mrs Whittle, the wife of the marine Sergeant Thomas Whittle, gave birth to a son on 26 January 1788. He was the first white child born in the new colony.

UNCHAINED

At first the convicts were chained. But chained men could do little work, so the chains were removed. Many convicts

immediately fled into the bush, hoping to reach the French ships in Botany Bay and be taken back home. But the French refused to help the escapees.

In those first years, many convicts escaped into the bush, hoping to walk overland to China or India: hardly any of them had a clue where they were. However, the bush was terrifying, and even flogging was preferable to starvation, so one by one most of the escapees straggled back—to be flogged for their disobedience.

WELCOMING THE WOMEN

By 6 February all the male convicts had left the ships. Then the women convicts were rowed ashore. Despite the squalor of their lives on board ship, most of them had tried to keep clean clothes for this occasion. They had even helped each other do their hair.

A ration of rum was given out to all to celebrate. But before the party could get going a violent storm lashed the tents, with a lightning flash that destroyed a tree in the camp, killing the sheep and pig that were sheltering under it. Finally the storm died down, and the rest of the night was filled with singing and drunken quarrels.

And, probably, within a few days there were hardly any women who hadn't found a partner to help them build a shelter, even if it was just one of the sailors who would soon be leaving.

WHERE ARE ALL THE CHICKS?

The colony had everything from wheelbarrows to hinges, from glue to parsnip seed. But one thing it didn't have was enough women. By one count there were 548 male convicts, 247 marines, 188 female convicts and about 5 wives of marines (officers and privates weren't allowed to bring their wives). How would the colony produce children, who would grow into new colonists, without enough women?

There had been hopes that some of the Indigenous women would be willing to marry convict men, but none stepped forward. The British Government had ordered Phillip to fetch more women from Polynesia, but the plan had to be dropped. If the colony couldn't feed its own people, how could it feed another five hundred Polynesian women?

Where were the extra women to come from?

WHAT TO WEAR?

The women were given new clothing before they left England: 4 white shifts; 1 grey jacket (more like a blouse than a coat); 1 white jacket; 2 checked jackets; 1 woollen jacket; 2 canvas petticoats; 2 linsey-woolsey petticoats; 1 serge petticoat; 3 handkerchiefs; 2 caps; 1 hat; 3 pairs of stockings; 3 pairs of shoes.

The men were given: 2 jackets; 4 woollen drawers (pants); 1 hat; 3 shirts; 4 pairs of worsted stockings; 3 frocks (like long gathered shirts); 3 trousers; 3 pairs of shoes.

These clothes were supposed to last them two years.

Work? Us? You're Kidding!

Convicts were not the best settlers. Many were city people, and they were scared of both the sounds and the silence of the new land.

Most were people who had chosen a life of crime rather than of work. After the first few weeks, Governor Phillip worked out that only one in every three convicts would be willing to work. So Phillip laid down harsh laws: if the convicts didn't work, they wouldn't eat. And anyone stealing food or animals would be hanged.

Convicts were put into gangs, and they elected their own foremen. The marines refused to supervise these work-gangs. They said that they were soldiers, sent to guard the colony, not to be policemen or convict supervisors. So convicts were appointed as policemen as well.

The Gaol without Walls

The convicts were still prisoners, but their only real prison walls were the sea and the bush. Unless the convicts committed new crimes, they were neither locked up nor made to work in leg-irons. And when they had done their assigned work they were free to work their own gardens— if they could be bothered. It was a mess of a system. But it was the best that Governor Phillip could do.

Takeaway Tripe

Back in London, most of the poor lived close to starvation. Even if they had a stove to cook on, most Londoners couldn't afford the fuel. Wood was scarce and coal was expensive.

So poor Londoners would eat takeaways from shops that sold tripe, pies or faggots (animal innards mixed with fat and oatmeal, then baked); from eel or oyster stalls; from trays or wheelbarrows of roasted chestnuts and hot potatoes; or—if they had a bit of cash—in taverns. The very poor lived on bread or gruel, which was made of oats and flour boiled in water. The poorer you were, the more watery your gruel.

I'll have gruel, please, with a side of gruel, and gruel for dessert.

For this reason, many of the convicts had no idea how to cook, much less how to grow vegies or hunt. But they would have to learn how to cook if they wanted to eat in the colony!

HOW TO MAKE 1788 DAMPER

Ingredients:

Flour (including weevils for protein)

Water (fresh)

Preparation:
1. Collect dry wood and build a fire

2. Mix the flour and water

3. Shape dough into a flat cake

4. Allow fire to burn down to hot coals

5. Shovel hot coals away and place dough on hot earth

6. Shovel hot coals back on top of the dough

7. Sing a dozen choruses (or wait 20 minutes)

Singing Too-rall, li-oo-rall, li-addity Singing...

8. Remove damper from under coals

9. Allow to cool

10. Dust off excess ash

11.

TAKE YOUR PICK

Each male convict was given a spade, a shovel, a felling axe, three hoes and a hatchet. This was so they could clear land and grow food. They were also given a knife and pannikin for cooking; a wooden bowl, platter and spoon for eating; and gimlets for boring through wood.

THE FOUL FRENCH

Meanwhile, the French were still at Botany Bay. But while the British had tried to make friends with the Cadigal, the French built a stockade and fired on them. The Cadigal probably couldn't tell the difference between the French and the British. Both had arrived in big ships. Both had white faces and strange clothes. So, even though the British hadn't fired on them, the British (like the French) must be enemies too.

La Pérouse and his men stayed at Botany Bay for six weeks. Then they sailed away, never to return. The ships were wrecked in the New Hebrides soon after, with all hands lost.

Eora Backlash

The Eora people had at first been friendly towards the new colonists. But by early February things had changed. What went wrong? Did the Eora have bad experiences with the French? Or did they realise that the British were going to stay, and not sail away like last time? Were they angry about the tree-clearing, the fishing and the shooting of kangaroos? Or were they retaliating for crimes the convicts had committed against them?

The colony's convicts made bad neighbours. They stole Eora tools, canoes and weapons and sold them to the marines and sailors. (Phillip made it illegal to sell tools or canoes stolen from the Eora, but the law was ignored.) An Eora man was peppered with shot when he tried to take some tools. Another was killed in a fight with convicts. Then two convicts cutting rushes were killed by Eora. A party of surveyors was forced to run when they met a crowd of Eora men brandishing spears.

The native people of the USA were called *Indians* because Christopher Columbus thought he had landed in India. The marines who had fought in the American War of Independence called the native Australians *Indians* too.

Phillip and a dozen armed men tried to make peace, but they were met by about two hundred armed Eora. After that, Phillip ordered that no-one was to go into the bush alone. They had to travel in parties of at least six, and be armed as well. However, Phillip believed that the Eora only acted in self-defence—or else to protect their tools, fishing nets, canoes or women—so he ordered that no-one was allowed to fire on the Eora unless the situation was desperate.

But the situation grew worse. Two convicts gathering wild greens were attacked in July. A sailor who was lost in the bush was stoned by Eora, but when he pointed a stick at his attackers, pretending it was a musket, he was able to escape.

By October attacks had become frequent. One day some Eora threw spears at a convict who was on his way to a newly fenced stockyard. Governor Phillip headed for the spot with an armed party, even though the convict hadn't been hurt. They could hear the Eora in the bushes and Phillip ordered the troops to open fire. He hoped this would frighten the Eora into keeping away from the settlement.

WILL WE ALL BE KILLED?

This certainly wasn't the land of a few scattered local people that Sir Joseph Banks had described. The Eora outnumbered the new settlers by at least two to one. They knew the land, and the newcomers didn't.

The colonists' only advantage was their muskets and cannons. When the gunpowder ran out, the settlers would be helpless.

Captain Cook had been ordered by the British authorities to make a treaty with the native people of New Holland. This treaty was meant to be an agreement that would let the British newcomers use the land. But Cook didn't follow these orders.

Governor Phillip also had his orders: to treat the Aboriginal population with kindness and consideration. Governor Phillip was a kind and considerate man, and he was fascinated by the Aboriginal culture. He hoped to show the Eora that the new settlers were friendly . . . and then he intended to show them how superior the British settlers were.

Remember, soldiers, invade this beach with kindness and consideration.

But many of the new settlers were *not* friendly. *Or* superior!

WHY NO TREATY?

The British Government later signed treaties with the Maoris of New Zealand. But they never offered a treaty to the Aboriginal people of Australia.

The Aboriginal people didn't fight the newcomers the way the Maori did. The Maori fought the kind of organised battles that the British understood, but the Aboriginal people made small attacks on isolated farms, or on people who had wandered away from the settlement.

Furthermore, the Eora didn't own the land in a way that could be signed away in a treaty. The Eora shared the land between them, and they had special duties towards it . . . and the new settlers didn't understand this at all.

A treaty is a formal agreement between countries or governments. A treaty is often about the ways in which the two parties negotiate peace.

Great Ambitions

Meanwhile, a stone house was going up for the governor, and wooden storehouses and barracks had been built. The women convicts collected shells for making lime to cement bricks from the new brickworks.

Convict bricks were uneven and crumbly, and there was so little mortar that most bricks were cemented with a mix of mud and wool, which washed out in the first big storms.

Oooh! Look at this pretty one.

DEATH BY INDIGESTION
One convict made up his entire week's ration of flour into eighteen cakes. He ate them at one sitting—and died, vomiting and stinking, the next day.

In April Sydney Town was marked out by the surveyors. Even though it was still a town of ragged tents, the main street was about sixty metres wide. Who knew, perhaps Sydney Town might one day be a major city of the British Empire!

But for the time being, the tents leaked, the privies stank, and the Tank Stream was already muddy and smelly.

And now winter was coming.

How to Eat Your Rations

Forget about boiling your salt pork—it's four years old, black, too hard to cut, and shrinks by half when it's cooked! Instead, toast your whole week's ration on a stick over the fire, and catch the drips of fat on a bit of damper. And why bother making damper every day? Boil your flour ration with wild greens, and gulp the sour porridge down when it cools.

Governor Phillip noted that the Eora people politely took bread or salted meat when it was offered to them. He also noted that they usually threw it away. But if they were offered fresh fish they ate it!

A Land of Loneliness

The new colonists were eight months' sail away from everyone they knew and loved. The wives of convicts sometimes asked to be allowed to join their husbands in Sydney Town, but very few were given permission. There were almost no complete families in the colony.

The marines had mostly left their families behind too. Only sergeants and corporals were allowed to bring their wives and children with them. Officers weren't allowed to, although Major Ross (who was Governor Phillip's stubborn and demanding second-in-command) cheated a bit and brought his son as a volunteer. Ross later made his son a Second Lieutenant, even though the boy was only nine years old!

Even when free settlers started to arrive, there were always more men than women. Many men would never marry or have a family. There just weren't enough women to go around. For many decades the colony was full of cranky, bitter— and mostly drunk— bachelors.

In Dublin's fair city, where the girls are so pretty,...sob, sob.

CHAPTER 6

HARD TIMES

The first winter was hard. Most people still lived in leaky tents. There were no blankets or sheets for the hospital. The wheat, maize and vegetables had been planted too late to get a proper harvest, and much of the wheat and barley didn't even germinate.

Phillip's dream was that each person in the colony would grow most of their own food—just as cottagers did back in Britain, with vegetable gardens for potatoes and greens. There were tools and seeds and as much land as anyone wanted, so long as they were prepared to chop down the trees and grub out the roots and the tussocks. But many of the convicts deliberately broke their tools, or else lost them, to avoid having to work. Their lives depended on what they could grow—but many failed to realise it.

Two bulls and four cows wandered away, and all but one of the sheep wandered off as well—no-one had bothered to tend them.

Black Caesar was an escaped African-West Indian slave who became a pickpocket—and then a convict on the First Fleet. He was a giant of a man, and the hardest worker in the colony. He was also a big eater, and stole to get extra food. He escaped to the bush in 1789, and terrorised the colony with daring night raids. When he was caught again a few months later Phillip put him to work in the vegetable gardens at Garden Island—with extra vegetables to eat! Black Caesar escaped four more times. In 1796 a settler named Winbow tracked him down and shot him in return for a reward of 23 litres of rum!

Suddenly, and mysteriously, there were fewer fish in the harbour. The Eora twice attacked one of the colony's fishing boats and took fish when the sailors wouldn't share the catch. The shortage of fish had left the Eora hungry too.

The hospital began to fill with scurvy patients, who were sick from not eating enough fresh fruit and vegetables. Their teeth fell out, their gums bled, and they grew too weak to stand.

STARVED TO DEATH

A convict was found dead in the bush near the settlement. When Mr Balmain, the Assistant Surgeon, opened the man up to find out why he'd died, he found that the convict's stomach was totally empty. The poor man hadn't eaten for a week. He had been saving his rations to sell them, so that he could buy a passage back to England once he'd served his sentence.

CAN'T BE BOTHERED

New Holland was actually a land of abundance. The Eora probably had to work less for their food than most other people on earth. To them, every tree was a supermarket—nectar-rich blossom to suck; insects to eat; wild honey and possums in the hollows; birds' eggs in the nests; young sweet roots to roast in the ashes. There was food everywhere—but you had to know how to find it. And you had to be prepared to eat it!

Or you had to work for it. The Sydney land is fertile and the climate is great for crops.

I've found something!

Some of the colony's gardeners dusted their plots with ash, made compost, and spread what little manure there was. But many didn't bother to grub out all the tree and grass roots before they planted. They didn't even bother watering or weeding.

The colonists tried to tame dingoes to help them hunt. But the dogs stayed savage, even when brought up from puppies.

Most of the convicts would rather steal—or starve—than do the hard work needed to keep a garden. And those marines who had gardens of their own—worked with convict labour—only grew enough food for themselves.

ABANDONED!

The first of the ships that had brought the convicts left Sydney Town on 14 July 1788—the *Alexander*, the *Prince of Wales*, the *Friendship* and the storeship *Borrowdale*. By now a new storeship should have arrived from England with fresh supplies. But none came. Phillip sent a party down to Botany Bay to put up notices saying that the colony had moved up the coast—just in case a ship arrived expecting to find them and didn't know where they'd gone.

In September Phillip sent the *Sirius* to Cape Town to fetch supplies. But it might take as much as six months for her to return with food. She was meant to fetch wheat seed, too, as almost all the seed the colonists had brought with them had gone bad. Half a kilogram of flour was deducted from everyone's rations so that the food would last longer.

On 19 November the *Fishburn* and the *Golden Grove* sailed back to England. Now the colony only had one ship left—the tiny *Supply*.

The colonists were cut off from the world.

DESPERATE AND DEAD

Because of the food shortages, parties of convicts walked as far as Botany Bay to find wild greens. They were guarded by soldiers to keep them safe from 'Indians', but one convict, Cooper Handley, wandered away from the rest. His body was found with his head beaten to a pulp, a spear through his skull, another through his body, and his arm broken.

THE COLONY'S FIRST FREE SETTLER

James Smyth (or Smith) bought a passage to New Holland on the *Lady Penrhyn*. He said that he had farming experience, and hoped to find a good job in the new colony. He was given a job as an assistant in the food store; then he was put in charge of the Rose Hill Farm. But according to the Governor's Secretary, Collins, Smyth was too 'advanced in years', and he also couldn't control the convicts. So he lost his job.

MAJOR ROSS THE MAJOR ROTTER

The marines—and their commander, Lieutenant-Governor Major Ross—were getting restless. With no French to fight, they had little to do. They were bored. Fights broke out, and quarrels, even murders. Where was the grog they had been promised—and proper food?

Ross had sent angry letters to his superiors in England via the returning convict transports. He complained that it was impossible for the troops to drink water instead of wine, and demanded that three years' worth of wine and spirits be sent to the colony at once. He also complained that he was only given 170 grams of butter a week—which was the same as what the convicts got! He also refused to have his marines do any extra work—not even building their own barracks—unless they got extra pay. Major Ross even said that Governor Phillip was lying about how great Sydney Town was.

Phillip says he has very nice views of the harbour.

Ross doesn't even mention the view.

According to Major Ross, this 'vile country' was the worst in the world. It was barren and back to front; a place where seed rotted when it was put into the ground; a wretched country that would never support a settlement! Ross said it would be cheaper to feed convicts on turtle soup and venison back in London than send them to Port Jackson!

So many marines wrote letters that exaggerated how bad things were in the colony that when Major Grose arrived in 1792, he expected to find a barren rock. Instead he was startled to find flourishing gardens and fruit trees!

Things Improve—a Bit

Things grew better once spring and summer came. Those orchards and vegetable gardens that were well-tended soon flourished. The fresh produce meant that scurvy and dysentery patients recovered and could do some work. But most gardens weren't looked after and grew more weeds and caterpillars than vegetables.

Governor Phillip declared that the maize crops were as good as any in the world. But both the convicts and the marines refused to eat maize flour. They wanted the flour they had known all their lives—wheat flour.

Good farming land was found upriver at Rose Hill (Parramatta). It was so rich that it grew crops even without fertiliser. But despite the supply of maize and other vegetables, discontent and hunger grew worse. Thefts were frequent. Phillip ordered that any convict who stole would get only a canvas frock and trousers to wear, and that if convicts didn't do a proper day's work they would get only two-thirds of their normal rations.

FALSE ALARM!

In December a messenger came running to say that two thousand Eora armed with spears had gathered at the brickworks about a mile from the main settlement of Sydney Cove. Then a second messenger arrived and said that there were actually only four hundred armed Eora.

> By 1789 four convicts had been killed by the Eora, and many more had been attacked.

An officer got together a small party of soldiers and raced to the rescue. But they found only fifty Eora—and when the convicts pointed their spades at them the Eora ran off.

They've all behind that bush.

How Many Eora Were There?

We will never know how many Eora there were when the British arrived. So many of them died in such a short time. Phillip thought there were about 1500 in the Sydney region, but there may have been several thousand.

KIDNAP!

Major Ross urged that the colony build a stockade, with defences against a massed attack by the Eora. But Governor Phillip had a different plan: he decided that some of the Eora should be kidnapped. This would either

force the Eora to attack *en masse*, so that the British could fight them properly in a proper battle; or else the kidnapped people would be so impressed by their captors' kindness that they'd go back and tell their people that the colonists were friendly. No-one seems to have mentioned to the governor that kidnapping wasn't a great way of showing friendliness.

ARABANOO

On 30 December 1788 two boatloads of soldiers were sent to Manly Cove to capture some 'Indians'. They managed to catch hold of two. One of them dragged his captor into deep water and escaped. But the other young man was bundled into the boat and taken back to the settlement at Sydney Cove.

The whole settlement turned up to look at the new prisoner. The crowd of yelling sightseers upset him, but he impressed the people with his dignity.

For a while Governor Phillip called him Manly, because that was where he'd been captured. But his real name was Arabanoo.

Arabanoo was scrubbed so his captors could see how dark his skin was. His hair and beard were cut. They were

full of lice and the prisoner seemed glad to be rid of them. He started to eat the lice, but when the soldiers looked disgusted, he stopped. Then he was dressed in English clothes and an iron handcuff was fastened to his wrist, with a rope attached. At first Arabanoo thought this was a gift of jewellery. He was furious when he discovered that its purpose was to tie him up.

Arabanoo had midday dinner with the governor, and ate the fish and duck that he was served—but he wouldn't eat the salt meat or the sour bread, and he spat out the grog.

Arabanoo was kept tied up for nearly five months. A convict accompanied him wherever he went as he wandered about the settlement—and even slept beside him, holding onto Arabanoo's rope to make sure he didn't escape.

At first he ate enormous meals: for example, eight big fish for breakfast, and for the main midday meal three kangaroo rats and two more big fish. Arabanoo was accustomed to feasting when there was a lot of food around, so that it didn't go to waste. But when he found out that food arrived regularly, he began to eat less. He made friends easily, especially with children, and always shared the best bits of his meal with them.

Three days after Arabanoo's capture, Phillip took him in a boat back to Manly Cove. Arabanoo's friends gathered nearby. Arabanoo wept, pointing at his chain to explain why he couldn't escape, and told them he was being held prisoner at Wee-rong—or Sydney Cove. Perhaps he was hoping that his friends would rescue him.

But once he was back at the settlement, his usual good humour returned, and he ate two kangaroo rats and three pounds of fish for dinner.

Two days later Phillip took him down to the harbour to talk to his countrymen again. But after this second visit, Arabanoo's people refused to talk to him. He stayed in the British settlement, lonely and alone except for the children who flocked around him.

And the attacks by the Eora—and the convicts—continued.

Starving in the Land of Plenty

By early 1789 those who had gardens—and could guard them—were eating well. Many of the gardens produced bigger vegetables than anyone had ever seen—massive potatoes, giant cabbages, radishes, turnips, beans, peas, tomatoes, endive, melons, cucumbers, pumpkins, strawberries, rhubarb and spinach. Fruit trees grew so quickly that in two years, apples, oranges, figs, grapes and pomegranates were bearing fruit.

The colony's hens had produced chickens, and those chickens were now in turn laying eggs; and there were more oysters and wild spinach than anyone could gather.

Fish were plentiful in summer. There was meat from kangaroos, parrots, wallabies, emus, kangaroo rats, echidnas and possums. Some people ate crows, ducks, swans, and wild eggs as well.

The colony's chief fisherman, convict William Bryant, was caught selling stolen fish. But his fishing skills were so valuable to the colony that there was little that could be done to punish him— except for making him abandon his hut.

But most people didn't have gardens. And now that so many people were shooting and trapping, there were fewer animals around. Many had also been scared away. Furthermore, powder for the muskets was now in short supply—and once the powder ran out the muskets were useless, both for hunting and for protection against the Eora. The colony had bullet moulds for melting down lead and making more bullets, but there would be no more powder till the *Sirius* returned from the Cape of Good Hope.

Most people still relied on the government-issued rations. And the remaining supplies—old and rancid as they were—were running desperately short. Furthermore, in March 1789, six marines were hanged for stealing food from the government stores. They'd been doing it for some time—which meant that there was actually much less food left in the stores than Governor Phillip had thought.

The colony had its rations cut by a third.

GROWLING AND GRUMBLING

Food was precious, and the rations alone weren't enough to do hard work on. But most convicts were probably eating better than they had ever eaten before. After all, they had almost starved in England. They were also healthier than ever before, working in the fresh air and the sunlight. But they were often hungry; and even hungrier for the food they were familiar with, in particular, meat and bread and grog.

The marines were hungry too—and angry. They expected to eat enormous amounts of beef, pork or mutton three times a day, accompanied by bread and tarts and puddings. Vegetables were simply not real food at all.

CHAPTER 7

PESTS, POX AND PLAGUE

On April 15 1789 a party of men who were cutting grass trees found a sick Eora man and boy, and another boy dead. They took the sick people back to the hospital, where the surgeon decided they had smallpox—a deadly disease that left its sufferers with sores all over their body.

But was it smallpox? It looked just like it—but it was the strangest plague that any of the colonists had ever seen, because only the Eora died—and one Native American sailor.

Hundreds died. Their bodies floated on the waves in the harbour, as though the sick had tried to cool their fever in the water. Others died in the caves in the cliffs, with purple faces and sores all over their bodies.

Where had this disease come from? The Eora called it *gal-gal-la*. Did this mean they knew the disease and had suffered from it before? Had the new settlers brought

We will never know for certain how many Eora died of this mystery disease, but estimates are between fifty and ninety percent of the Eora population.

it—but if so, why weren't any of them sick? Had the French brought it? Or other earlier explorers?

The sick people were brought in to the settlement by their friends; others were picked up in the Governor's boat, and the hospital did its best to care for them. Two Eora children survived the disease—a boy called Nanbaree, and a girl called Boorong.

The colony's doctors had brought smallpox scabs with them, which they kept in bottles in the hospital to be used for inoculation. But no-one thought the plague had come from these scabs.

THE DEATH OF ARABANOO

Arabanoo nursed the sick Eora children, but he caught the disease from them and fell sick too. The surgeons tried desperately to save him because by now the gentle Arabanoo was greatly loved in the settlement. But after six days of illness he died. Governor Phillip watched as Arabanoo was buried in the governor's garden.

Nanbaree was adopted by Surgeon White. He is probably the one who showed his adoptive father many of the local medicinal plants that White later recorded. Boorong was adopted by the Reverend Richard Johnson and his wife.

Suddenly the beautiful harbour was empty—there were no more women fishing in their canoes, with their tiny fires on board and the children swimming in the waves. Most of the surviving Eora seemed to have fled inland to escape the disease.

But the resistance to the newcomers continued. The governor decided it was time for another kidnap.

BENNELONG AND COLBEE

On 25 November 1789 Lieutenant Bradley and some other armed officers rowed across to the north of the harbour. Some Eora were walking on the beach, and Bradley offered two young men some fish to entice them into the boat. As soon as the young men stepped aboard they were seized and tied up. The men's friends raised their spears ready to attack, but they stopped when the officers raised their muskets.

Nanbaree and Boorong ran down to the shore to greet the boat in Sydney Cove, yelling out the captives' names—Bennelong and Colbee. Colbee, a Cadigal man, was Nanbaree's uncle, and Nanbaree had already told Surgeon White what a great warrior and leader Colbee was.

The men were taken to the governor's house, where they were shaved, washed and dressed, just as Arabanoo had been. Each was also made to wear an iron leg-shackle with a rope attached which was held by a convict guard.

The first night, Bennelong and Colbee were locked in a room at the governor's house. They chewed through their ropes, but as they didn't know how to unlock the door or windows, they weren't able to escape.

Colbee managed to get away soon afterwards—and his convict keeper was given a hundred lashes for letting him escape. Then the rope on Bennelong's shackle was replaced by a metal chain, which was in turn chained to the leg of his convict keeper.

Bennelong seemed happier once Colbee was gone. He was younger than Colbee, and not as respected by his own people, so with Colbee no longer around he felt free to laugh and joke.

> Bennelong's wife had died of smallpox. Bennelong also caught the disease, but he recovered.

Bennelong was genuinely curious about the white settlers, and a strange friendship soon developed between Governor Phillip and the captive. Both were lonely: Bennelong because he was imprisoned and separated from his people; the governor because of the heavy responsibility of running a colony at the end of the earth. They took walks together; they ate dinner together. Bennelong called the governor *beanga,* or father, and freely told Governor Phillip about his society and culture. The shackle was taken off Bennelong's leg in April 1790, which left him free to take even longer walks with the governor.

BENNELONG THE KIDNAPPER

Unlike Arabanoo, Bennelong enjoyed alcohol, and drank whatever was offered. He also boasted of forcibly abducting a woman from another tribe and beating her insensible.

TUCKER TIME AT LAST!

The *Sirius* returned from Cape Town in May 1789. She brought the first news of the outside world since the ships had left England in 1787.

But she only brought four months' supply of flour. It was all she could carry!

And it wasn't enough.

However, the *Sirius* also brought more seed. The summer crops at Rose Hill and the colony's other vegetable gardens had been excellent. However, the maize crop was a disaster: in a single night, rats had eaten almost every cob, and those cobs that weren't eaten proved to have no kernels anyway. Nearly every night a garden was robbed of its crop. In September the colony ran out of butter. In October the rations were cut again by another third. By December the gardens were cropping again after winter, but most of the wheat and corn was needed to feed the animals.

> When the colony's livestock had offspring, most of them were male. One sow had twelve piglets, but only three of them were girl pigs!

Guardian on the Rocks

The colonists felt as though England had forgotten them. But this wasn't the case. As soon as the Colonial Office in England received the letters from the returning convict ships, a ship called the *Guardian* was equipped with everything the colony had asked for—and more. The Colonial Office even provided a special plant room for transporting fruit trees, grape vines, artichoke plants and herbs—as well as enough clothes and goods to last four or five years. The *Guardian* also carried skilled convicts such as farmers, blacksmiths, shoemakers and an engineer, just as Phillip had requested.

The *Guardian* sailed on 8 September 1789. The captain loaded nine thousand litres of wine at Tenerife, more animals at Cape Town (including every sort of poultry he could find) and 150 varieties of trees.

But two weeks out from Cape Town the *Guardian* hit an iceberg. She was driven ashore and shattered. A few stores were saved and loaded onto the *Lady Juliana*, a convict transport that was sailing with the *Guardian*. But most of the cargo was lost.

But we can't just abandon the artichokes!

RUSE OF ROSE HILL

James Ruse was a convict, but had once been a farmer in Cornwall, England. When his sentence expired in July 1789 he was given two acres of land and a small hut at Rose Hill. Right from the beginning he was determined to show that a man could grow enough food to feed his family in the new colony.

He spread wood ash on the ground, and made compost out of rotted weeds and plant waste to use as fertiliser. By 1791 he refused to accept any more rations for himself and his family. As a reward for being so industrious, Governor Phillip gave him twelve hectares. This was the first land grant in Australia. By 1819 Ruse had over eighty hectares. But bad luck and rum eventually ruined him.

He lost his farm and ended up working as an overseer for another farmer.

The Moaning Major

Major Robert Ross hated the colony and its governor, and he took every chance to blacken the reputation of both. His own men, the marines, disliked him, and the convicts feared him. But he did his best to demand better conditions for his men. For example, why should the convicts be flogged with the 'cat-o'-nine-tails', and not the harsher 'military cat' that was used on marines? And how dare Governor Phillip stop the rum ration to the marines' wives?

In March 1790 Governor Phillip ordered Major Ross to take the *Sirius*, the *Supply* and a group of marines and convicts to Norfolk Island. The *Sirius* was to then go on to China to fetch more food. It was a way of getting rid of the troublesome Major Ross, as well as of reducing the number of mouths to feed in Sydney Town.

But while the *Sirius* was being unloaded at Norfolk Island, strong winds dashed it onto a reef. No-one died—but the loss of the *Sirius* meant that there would be no fresh food supplies from China. Now the colony's only ship was the tiny *Supply*. She had room for no more than fifty people. When would another ship arrive?

The convicts who were sent to rescue the pigs and other goods from the wreck of the *Sirius* got drunk instead.

Honk!

Weekly Rations, April 1790

The following rations were given to every man, convict or marine. The rations were handed out every day to stop the convicts eating their week's worth of food in one go.

1 kg flour, three years old, sour with weevils

1 kg salt pork—so hard and black you had to saw at it with a knife, *or*

4.5 kg fresh fish

1 cup wriggling rice *or*

500 g crumbling dried pease

Oatmeal, hard tack, cheese, butter and vinegar had by this time run out.

BAD TO WORSE!

By 1790 tools were scarce. Many had been lost, and others had broken or worn out. Many of the convicts were going barefoot. The colony had run out of candles, new clothes and many other of the necessities for a civilised life. People were getting thin.

The paintings and sketches of the time show officers in neat uniforms.
In reality they were ragged, with even their shoes falling off their feet.

Even worse, the colony was cut off from the world. What was happening to families left behind? Depression, anxiety and uncertainty gripped the colony in these early years. And they were hungry too!

In April 1790 Phillip sent the *Supply* to Batavia to buy more food. It would take the tiny ship at least six months to get there and back. Would she make it safely? Now that the *Sirius* had been wrecked and the other ships were gone, the colony had no way of escape if things got unbearable. They didn't even have a way of telling the rest of the world they were in trouble . . . or of sending stores to Norfolk Island.

The colony had only enough meat to last till the end of August. Rice and pease would run out in September, and flour in December. If all went well, the *Supply* might be back by the beginning of October. But by then the colony might have starved.

The marines had sworn never to supervise the convicts. Hunger finally forced them to change their minds, and they agreed to supervise the convicts on fishing parties, using private boats owned by the officers. The first such trip brought in 200 kilograms of fish. But after that the catches grew smaller, and the private owners took back their boats.

The colony's gunpowder was nearly gone. How were people going to hunt without gunpowder? The Eora knew how to hunt with spears and traps, but the colonists didn't.

FLOGGINGS FOR FOOD

Food was like gold, and was continually guarded by its owners against theft. A man called William Lane was sentenced to two thousand lashes for stealing biscuit; Thomas Halford got two thousand lashes for stealing 1.4 kilograms of potatoes; William Parr got five hundred lashes for stealing a pumpkin. A fisherman was given a hundred lashes for keeping some of the catch for himself.

WE'D RATHER STARVE!

In April 1790 Phillip decided that the convicts should only work for a few hours in the morning. They simply didn't get enough food to be able to work any longer—unless, of course, they had gardens of their own. Governor Phillip encouraged the convicts to start their own gardens and even showed them how to garden himself, but many of them would still rather go hungry than work.

DOBBER'S DELIGHT

In May Phillip announced that anyone who dobbed in a food thief would be rewarded with twenty-seven kilograms of flour. This was an enormous amount, when the ration was just over one kilogram a week. Even so, Governor Phillip's garden was still robbed almost every night.

Stuffed to Death

A female convict was so hungry she boiled up all her flour with as many greens as she could gather. She ate as much as she could during the day, then woke up in the night and ate the rest. The effect on her empty stomach was disastrous, and she died.

Two convicts fainted from hunger in the food queue and later died. One of them had lost his cooking tools, and his mates had demanded a share of his rations before they'd let him use their pots. So, in order to keep all his rations for himself, he tried to eat his rice raw—and the combination of hunger and indigestion killed him.

Can it Get any Worse?

The supply of pease ran out. Governor Phillip put his own store of flour into the common store and received only the same rations as everyone else. The only person who continued to eat well was Bennelong. Governor Phillip ordered that Bennelong receive extra fish and corn so that he wouldn't realise what a desperate state the colony was in. If the Eora realised how weak the colonists were (and knew how little gunpowder there was left) they might attack in force.

But then Bennelong escaped! At 2 am on 3 May he pretended to be sick. He woke up his convict guard and asked to go downstairs. Then he jumped over a paling fence and escaped. But things were so bad that Governor Phillip didn't even worry about it!

Clothes were nearly worn out, and winter was coming. Sentries stood guard duty in bare feet. Building work almost stopped. All the workers' energy was kept for growing their vegetables (or stealing other people's), collecting firewood or boiling salt from seawater to preserve meat the hunters brought in.

> There weren't enough fishing lines left but a convict who had been a rope maker watched how the Eora made nets from the bark of a tree, and made new nets for the colony.

Why were there no ships from England? Had the colony at the end of the world been forgotten? Day after day the colonists stared out towards the flagpole at South Head, knowing that as soon as the soldiers stationed there saw a ship they'd raise the flag.

But no ship came.

How to Build a Wattle-and-Daub Hut.

1. Cut down at least twenty good-sized trees. Seven need to be taller than head height.

2. Chop off all their branches.

Daub is mud and *wattles* are small supple branches that can be woven to make a fence or wall. Australian wattle trees were named for their supple young trunks and branches.

3. Dig 9 holes and stand the trunks upright in them.

4. Use 3 tall tree posts to make the roof and ridge pole. Fasten with straps of wet leather to the top of the tall posts.

5. Cut lots of small wattle saplings.

6. Weave them in and out between the posts (don't forget a door).

7. Fill the gaps in the weave with daub.

8. For the roof, place 4 posts along the tops of the walls.

9. Then fasten the remaining 6 posts at angles to the ridge pole.

10. Twist more wattle between the roof beams.

11. Cover with bundles of reeds or long strips of waterproof bark. The best roofs are tiled with shingles.

Daub→

UP IN SMOKE

The only way to heat a house or cook indoors was to have a fire, and a fire needed a chimney or the house would fill up with smoke. But the bricks in the new colony were so crumbly that most of the chimneys collapsed. As a result many people had to cook on a fire outside.

CHAPTER 8

THE FOUL FLEET

For months the colonists had hoped for sails on the horizon—waiting for food, for news of the outside world, for a hint they hadn't been forgotten. Finally, on 3 June 1790 the *Lady Juliana* glided through the heads—too far away from the main settlement for anyone to hear the flapping of her sails or the cries of her sailors. Then the yell 'the flag's up!' rang through the colony. People ran into the streets yelling and weeping with happiness. They had not been forgotten!

> The officers demanded the mailbags as soon as they climbed on board, and opened their letters with trembling hands.

At last there'd be more hard salt beef, more weevilly flour; more clothes, boots, candles, fishhooks, gunpowder . . . and, even more importantly, news from home!

But the *Lady Juliana* was no storeship—she had brought over two hundred women convicts! Unlike the women on the First Fleet, many of these new arrivals were old and feeble, although they had been well looked after. Instead of working to help the colony survive, they would have to be cared for— useless mouths eating the colony's food.

A TEARY FAREWELL

Phillip ordered that most of these women be sent straight on to Norfolk Island, as that colony had a better food supply due to the many mutton birds. The Reverend Richard Johnson preached a sermon on board the ship before they went, calling on the women to repent. Many had been prostitutes in England, and onlookers claimed that the sermon moved many of the women to tears.

NEWS AT LAST!

The *Lady Juliana* also brought news. The colony finally heard how the storeship *Guardian* had been wrecked on an iceberg off the Cape of Good Hope. And the settlers found out that the Second Fleet, with another thousand convicts, would be arriving any day. How was the colony going to house so many new convicts, and in winter too? The tents were in rags and most of the huts were miserable and leaking. But at least there would be more supplies, because the Second Fleet included a storeship.

The Nightmare Ships

The storeship *Justinian* arrived on 20 June, ahead of the convict transports. The colony rejoiced: food at last! Things looked good! The *Lady Juliana* and the *Justinian* had also brought goods for sale—hats, glass, paper, and luxury foods such as tea or currants.

Seven hundred grams of flour was immediately added back to the rations, even though there were now extra mouths to feed. Three days later the next of the convict transports arrived. But even as the *Surprize* came through the Heads, its passengers were dying and their bodies were being thrown over the side. Corpses washed up on the beaches for weeks afterwards.

These ships brought death, not life.

No Pleasure Cruise!

The *Surprize* unloaded its pitiful cargo of thin and dying convicts. The portable hospital that had arrived on the *Justinian* was immediately filled. Four days later the *Neptune* and *Scarborough* entered Sydney Cove and began unloading— and the full horror of the situation burst upon the colony.

The filth and starvation of those ships stunned the waiting officers. They had seen war, death and hardship, but they had never seen a sight like this. The convicts of the Second Fleet had to be carried up on deck. Most of them were too weak to even stagger, and crawled about on their hands and knees, unable to rise. Their eyes were blinded by the light, and their skin was festering. Some died right there on deck. Others died as they were rowed ashore. The stench was unbelievable.

First Fleet convicts and women from the *Lady Juliana* who had relatives or friends on the Second Fleet tried desperately to find them. But the Second Fleeters were so starved, pale and filthy that no-one could recognise them, and no records had been kept as to who had been dumped over the side.

Don't Wash 'em, Burn 'em!

The convicts' clothes were so stiff with filth that they had to be burnt, even though the colony was short of cloth. The naked sick were wrapped in blankets while dressmakers frantically tried to make clothes for eight hundred convicts.

Emma! Skip embroidering the cuffs!

Seamstress

According to Governor Phillip, 267 people had died on the journey out. The surviving convicts were so hungry that many had chosen to remain chained to a dead companion in order to get that corpse's rations. Of the surviving 759 convicts, 488 were ill. This left only 271 healthy convicts. The marines, Governor Phillip and the Reverend Richard Johnson were horrified.

> Most of the convicts on the Second Fleet were dumped in crying heaps on the beach. Colonists had to carry them up to the hospital on their backs.

Thirty tents were put up beside the hospital. The patients were suffering scurvy, dysentery, starvation and a whole range of infectious fevers. As soon as one died, his or her blanket was stripped off and given to someone else. Another 124 convicts died almost straightaway.

How had this happened?

SECOND FLEET CHEATS

The First Fleet had been organised by the British Government and Captain Arthur Phillip. Phillip had been determined that he would bring his convicts to the new colony as healthy as possible. His ships' captains were fined £40 for every convict they lost.

The Second Fleet, however, was not organised by the government: it was organised by businessmen. These men paid the Second Fleet captains according to how many convicts they carried. This meant the more convicts the better—and it didn't matter how many were crammed into each ship, or if they starved to death on the way. Money was more important to these captains than convict lives. The Second Fleet convicts were kept below deck with the hatches battened down for the entire voyage and were chained together so they couldn't move.

The captains kept most of the food that was meant for the convicts. As soon as the ships landed, the captains opened these stolen stores to sell them to the hungry officers of Sydney Town. They sold them at the highest price that the desperate colonists were able to pay. Phillip was powerless to stop them—and the goods were soon sold. From this time on, most captains and shipowners would crowd the convicts onto their ships and starve them.

CROOKS FOR COPPERS

However, more than stores and convicts arrived with the Second Fleet. The New South Wales Corps landed too, under the command of Captain Nicholas Nepean. The Corps had been recruited especially to serve in New South Wales, and to do the tasks that the marines had refused to do—that is, to oversee the convicts and to serve as magistrates.

> A magistrate is an official person who presides over simple courts of law.

Many of the New South Wales Corps were crooks and rogues who had been thrown out of other regiments. Some were officers trying to run away from their debts, or who had stolen money from their fellow soldiers, or who had committed other crimes. These rogues had been offered a choice between being kicked out of the army—or going to the colony of New South Wales.

DECISIONS, DECISIONS!

There would now, for the first time, be regular ships going back and forth between England and the colony, as well as between the colony, India and China. The high prices that the colonists were willing to pay for food and alcohol meant that there was good money to be made by calling in to Sydney Town.

This meant that the privates and non-commissioned officers of the First Fleet had a choice: they could either travel back to England on one of these visiting ships, or they could take up a land grant. If they chose to stay and serve in the NSW corps, they would be offered a double land grant in five years' time. Male convicts who had served their sentences could also take up land, or else go back to England. However, most women weren't given land. They could either find a man to look after them, or sail back home!

Now, Be Honest!

All convicts sent to New South Wales had originally been sentenced to at least seven years. But some had been in jail for several years before the fleet sailed, so they became free—or emancipists—after only a couple of years in the colony. However, as Phillip wasn't supplied with any records about how long each of the convicts had served, he had no idea whether or not the men who claimed to have served their sentences really had!

What time does the next ship depart?

Have Some Land

Non-commissioned officers (such as sergeants and corporals) got 52 hectares; private soldiers got 32 hectares; if the soldier had a wife he got an extra 8 hectares; and for every child an extra 4 hectares. This land was free of rent for ten years, and after that a shilling a year for every twenty hectares.

Officers weren't given land grants. Maybe no-one thought that an officer would want to stay in the colony longer than he had to.

More *Nice* Settlers, Please

Now that there were ships coming and going, it was possible to send letters back to England. Not just letters to family and friends, but official letters too. Governor Phillip asked the British Government to send free settlers to the colony as soon as possible. The convicts, the governor explained, shrank from hard work and would therefore be of little use as settlers once their terms expired.

Settling down is way too much hard work!

How Do You D—*urgh!*

On 7 September 1790 Bennelong invited Phillip to a feast of whale meat at Manly. After landing in the cove, Phillip

walked through a group of armed Eora men to talk to Bennelong and Colbee, and to hand them some gifts. Bennelong demanded hatchets as well as the other gifts. Phillip promised to return in two days with the hatchets, and asked for a fine barbed spear in return. Bennelong gave Governor Phillip a throwing stick instead.

At first, everything seemed to be friendly. The armed men started moving towards Governor Phillip and Bennelong introduced him to several people. But when Phillip approached one of the men to greet him, a man called Wileemarin picked up a spear with his toes and threw it, hitting Phillip just above the collarbone.

Had the man been frightened? Was this a payback attack for the kidnapping of Bennelong and Colbee? We'll never know.

Will the Governor Die?

The weight of the spear pulling at Governor Phillip's flesh was unbearable, so one of his officers snapped it off. However, the barbed point remained in the wound.

Jolly fine throw!

Phillip staggered to the boat, in great pain and bleeding badly, and he was rowed the eleven kilometres back to Sydney Cove. Despite the agony from the spearhead still in his body, Phillip organised his affairs in case he died—and only then did he order the surgeon to dig out the spearhead. This was done with no anaesthetic, no blood transfusions, no antibiotics for infection—just a knife probing at the wound to dig out the barbs! Phillip didn't die, although the wound troubled him for the rest of his life.

A month later Bennelong called in to ask how the governor was, and from then on he visited the governor often, sometimes bringing his friends. Typically, the sensible Governor Phillip decided not to send soldiers to arrest the man who had speared him. He believed the spearing may have been the result of a misunderstanding, and with food and gunpowder in such short supply, he couldn't risk offending the Eora and inviting an attack.

SUPPLIES FROM THE *SUPPLY*

In October 1790 the *Supply* finally returned from Batavia, fully laden and with news that another ship, the *Waaksamheyd*, had been hired to bring more food to the hungry colony. There would still be many times when the colony was forced to buy food from overseas for convict rations—and there were still too many people that had to be fed at government expense—but the farms at Rose Hill were finally producing, and the fear of real starvation was finally over.

The brilliantly coloured birds that flocked to the grain fields at Rose Hill were called *Rose Hillers*—and that name became rosella! In 1791 Rose Hill became Parramatta— 'the place where eels lie down' or 'the head of the river'—named after the Burramattagal people who lived there.

PARRAMATTA MATTERS

There were now five hundred convicts working in the fertile Rose Hill settlement. Two hundred acres were being farmed, there were two main streets, brick houses for single convict men, more for single convict women, and cottages for married convicts. More land was continually being cleared for farming and fenced off for cattle. Rose Hill was doing so well it looked as though it would soon be New South Wales' capital, and Sydney Town just its port.

THE WARRIORS' REVENGE

In December 1790 Phillip's gamekeeper, McEntire, was speared and killed, probably by the Bidjigal warrior Pemulwuy. McEntire was serving a sentence for robbery, and was one of three convicts who had been given a musket to shoot game for the governor's table. He was feared for his bad temper, as well as for the musket he carried, and he was known to have killed at least one Eora man, and possibly also raped Eora women.

Governor Phillip had always tried to work out any problems with the Eora without using violence. But after the murder of McEntire his attitude hardened. He ordered a party of fifty-two soldiers to bring him the heads of ten Aboriginal people, as well as two live captives.

After discussion with Captain Tench (who was horrified), Governor Phillip relented and ordered that six be brought in alive instead. But the soldiers sent out to bring them in only saw Eora men running away on their first trip, and on their second could find no Eora men at all.

The Third Fleet of Thieves

The Third Fleet arrived between July and October 1791. Once again the captains and the shipowners had felt free to transport the convicts as cheaply as possible. This fleet had set out with two thousand convicts—but 194 men and four women had died on the voyage. More died soon after they reached shore. Conditions on the Third Fleet weren't as bad as they had been on the Second—but once again the colony had been sent people who needed care, nursing and food, instead of people who could help the colony survive. It seemed that no sooner did the colony get a little ahead, than another disaster was thrust upon it.

Passion for Rations

In December 1791 Governor Phillip ordered that rations be issued every day again, instead of every Saturday. When rations were issued once a week, many convicts stuffed themselves and often had nothing left by Wednesday. One of the reasons for this was that the convicts had no way of storing their food while they were away at work: in this settlement of huts and ragged tents and skilled thieves, how could they keep it safe?

In May 1792 the rations were cut—to 600 grams of flour, one kilogram of maize, two kilograms of pork per person per week, divided into portions for distribution each day. Women and children, of course, received less.

The officers of the New South Wales Corps were as hungry as everyone else. However, they had seen the enormous profits made by the captains of the Second and Third Fleets, so they set up a private company to hire a ship to import stores and sell them to their fellow colonists.

The More the Merrier

By 1792 there were about four thousand white settlers in Sydney Town and surrounding settlements—even though nearly five hundred people died in the winter of 1792 because so many of the new convicts had arrived weak and starving. Second and Third Fleet survivors were sometimes so weak that they took months to recover.

Now that there were so many more settlers, the terror that they might all be wiped out by hostile Eora also finally disappeared. The Eora were already outnumbered by white people. Scattered warfare would continue for more than a hundred years, but the nightmare that one day a ship might arrive to find the colony starved, or killed by hostile natives, was gone.

Over the next few years the colony had three main problems: the irregular arrival of more and more convicts who needed to be fed; flooding in the Hawkesbury River that ruined the crops; and the lack of silos to store the crops that survived the floods and droughts.

WHALE OF A TIME

When a whaling captain sighted a pod of whales a little way south of Port Jackson, it looked for the first time as though the colony might actually be profitable—there were more whales in this pod than the captain had ever seen. Whale oil was the source of great wealth at the time, as oil lamps were the only source of light for many houses.

CHAPTER 9

NORFOLK FOLK

Soon after Arthur Phillip arrived at Sydney Cove in 1788 he took swift action to grab Norfolk Island before the French could take it. He sent the *Supply* to the island with twenty-three men, of whom fifteen were convicts, under the leadership of Lieutenant Philip King. They took with them six months' worth of rations, and orders to start growing crops and harvesting and processing the flax to make sails.

Norfolk Island was a place of hardship—the harbours were dangerous, the huts leaked, the convicts had few clothes and little familiar food. They had to eat kangaroo rats, mutton birds, cabbage-tree hearts and chickweed. It was not as awful as being in an English prison, but in spite of King's glowing reports, and the island's rich soil and mild climate, the convicts felt they had been transported twice. Once from England. And again from New South Wales.

In January 1789 the convicts plotted to steal the *Supply* and sail her to Tahiti. The plot was foiled by a man who didn't want to go to Tahiti, but who was afraid his girlfriend would sail off with the plotters and leave him behind. So he dobbed the plotters in!

Lieutenant King went back to England in 1790.

Major Ross took over and divided the convicts into groups, each with their own patch of land. But most of the convicts refused to work. By May 1790 the colony was on short rations, despite the arrival of thousands of petrels on the island. On one night alone, the settlers killed about six thousand of the birds, eating some of them fresh and drying the meat of the remainder. But the petrels were followed by a plague of caterpillars that ate the crops.

Ross was very strict and cruel—and both the convicts and the marines complained of the savage floggings that he dished out to both prisoners and soldiers alike.

Lieutenant-Governor King's return as commandant in 1791 came as a great relief. He and his wife, Anna, set up a school and an orphanage for the children.

CONVICT KIDS

What was it like for convict kids? Pretty bad. Both boys and girls were sexually abused by adult convicts and marines. For a while, children were included in work parties. Child convicts were also given the same sort of punishment as adults— such as floggings.

THE FLAX OF LIFE

The British thought that the flax growing naturally on Norfolk Island could be woven into canvas for sails. But no-one on the island colony could work out how to do it. When Lieutenant King was in England he suggested that Captain George Vancouver, who was about to go on a round-the-world voyage, kidnap some flax experts from New Zealand. In 1792 Vancouver kidnapped two Maoris, Toogee and Hoodoo, from New Zealand, and put them on a ship bound for Norfolk Island.

But after a single frustrating hour, King realised that these men had no idea how to spin or weave flax. According to them, flax weaving was women's work! So Toogee and Hoodoo stayed as guests in King's house until King personally took them back to New Zealand in 1793.

In 1795 King left again due to illness. A number of officers of the Corps filled in until Major Joseph Foveaux was appointed as the Norfolk Island commandant in 1800.

Foveaux turned the island into a fortress of stone. Each convict had to break five cartloads of stone a day for buildings and roads. They worked in rain, they worked from dawn; any complaint earned twenty-five lashes and the second complaint earned fifty. Prisoners were tortured with shackles that were made smaller month by month until they bit into the flesh. Men were locked alone and naked in a water pit for forty-eight hours at a time—so that if they fell asleep they drowned. Things got so bad that convicts deliberately committed offences in order to escape the island—either by being hanged, or by being sent to Sydney for trial.

By 1803 Lord Hobart, the Secretary of State for the Colonies, ordered that the Norfolk Island colony be abandoned. It was too expensive, too far from Sydney, and had turned out to be useless for timber, flax, or as a base to thwart the French.

Most of the convicts and half the soldiers left in 1804. The free settlers were unwilling to be transferred to Van Diemen's Land, and stayed until 1808. Governor King also wanted to keep the island base to supply whalers, and for ships on their way to China.

Finally, in early 1814, the last of the buildings was burnt to prevent the French from using them. The remaining settlers were evacuated to New Norfolk on the Derwent River in Van Diemen's Land; then the last of the soldiers left, leaving only ruins, wild dogs, goats and pigs to show that there had been a colony.

But the island wasn't to be empty for long . . .

CHAPTER 10

THE RUM CORPS RULES

Governor Phillip left Sydney Town in December 1792. He was still suffering from his spear wound. The poor rations and the stress of his five years as Governor had also made him ill and exhausted.

Phillip had been a hard-working and determined governor, dreaming of a colony of farmers that would one day be a real part of the British Empire, and not just a dumping ground for convicts. If it hadn't been for him the First Fleet colonists might have arrived too weak to survive, and the colony might have starved.

Furthermore, if Phillip had been as aggressive towards the Eora as the French were at Botany Bay, Sydney Town might have been wiped out by angry Eora people within the first few months. But Governor Phillip had worked hard to stay friends with the local people.

Phillip left behind a colony of wooden houses, and even a few brick ones, instead of the ragged tents he'd started out with. There were public buildings such as the barracks and hospital; convict gangs were now working under the supervision of the New South Wales Corps; there were productive farms and regular visits by trading ships and whalers.

It is true that the colonists and the Eora were still far from understanding each other, but Phillip had done his best, with a good heart. Two Eora men even accompanied Governor Phillip back to England—Bennelong and Yemmerrawanie.

GROSE MISCONDUCT?

When Phillip sailed away, Major Grose took over. Grose was the commander of the New South Wales Corps, and once Phillip left he was the most senior officer in Sydney. Grose was easy-going. He pretended not to notice when his officers acted corruptly.

From then on, all complaints would be heard by a military officer instead of a magistrate. This made it almost impossible to complain against anyone in the Corps—which meant that the Corps could get away with all sorts of crimes, from rape to theft, and nothing would be done about it.

Phillip had taken great care in distributing rations, insisting on complete equality for everyone. But Grose ended this, so that all members of the Corps got an extra 1.5 kilograms of flour a week. To encourage farming, Grose also gave generous land grants to his men, as well as convicts to work the land.

A RUM JOB LOT

In 1793 the American trader, the *Hope*, arrived. The captain refused to unload any food until all his rum (34 000 litres of it) had been sold. The New South Wales Corps put their money together and bought it all. From then on, no-one except for the officers of the Corps was allowed to trade with visiting ships. As soon as the ships came into the harbour, officers of the Corps would row out, buy the entire cargo, and then sell it on to the colony at double or triple the price.

Officers were allowed to buy alcohol, too, and to sell it again for an immense profit. They let visiting captains know that the Corps could supply whaling and convict ships with food supplies for their onward voyage—so long as those ships paid them with rum instead of money.

ROTTEN TO THE CORPS

The Corps paymaster was in charge of all the funds. At this time the paymaster was the ambitious young Lieutenant John Macarthur. One of the first things Macarthur did in this job was get together with his fellow Corps officers and organise a ship to bring a special cargo of goods from South Africa. Much of this cargo was rum.

FUNNY MONEY

When the British Government set up the colony, it supplied the settlers with tools, seeds, medicine, paper and many other things. But they provided no money. Why would a jail need money? In the early years of the colony, food was used as a way of paying people. As the colony grew, visiting sailors brought coins from all around the world—Indian rupees, Spanish ducats, Dutch guilders. The Governor and the Corps paymaster also issued something called *promissory notes* that were used like money.

Now rum was used instead.

The New South Wales Corps bought rum from visiting ships at one shilling per litre, then diluted it with water and sold it for six shillings per litre. They often forced colonists to accept rum as payment for things, instead of paying them with money. Convicts also wanted rum. They would even refuse to work unless they were paid with it. Sometimes the Corps insisted on paying with useless things, such as dozens of woollen stockings.

The New South Wales Corps soon became known as the Rum Corps.

John
Macarthur.

RICHES FROM RUM

Many of the Corps officers established large farms with their illegal land grants. Lieutenant Macarthur took up forty hectares of the best land at Parramatta, and called it Elizabeth Farm after his wife. When sheep were shipped to the colony from India, the Corps officers bought them all before any one else had a chance, and put them on their own farms.

Many of the small landowners were ex-convicts (or emancipists). They often couldn't afford the expensive goods sold by the Rum Corps. But they couldn't buy goods from anyone else—so they went into debt. Then, in exchange for their debt, they had to give up their land—and the officers of the Rum Corps got even wealthier.

However, although the officers were growing rich with their illegal businesses and farms, the farms were also feeding the colony, and the Corps' trading ships were bringing badly needed supplies.

THE COLONY IN 1794

By 1794 members of the Corps were getting rich, but they were making the colony prosperous too. There was no longer any shortage of food—though sometimes fresh food for the convicts ran out. In fact when the American ship *Hope* arrived in 1794, the colony had so much food that no-one would buy its cargo of salted meat—although it had no trouble selling the alcohol to the Corps! The main shortages were now fresh meat, which couldn't be stored for long and was mostly kept for the officers. There was also sometimes a shortage of flour.

I steal one cucumber and you are going to punish me with vegetables the rest of my life!

The colony was becoming a settlement of small farms and rich acres. Even the huts and tents of Sydney Town were being replaced with a good-looking township of timber and stone buildings. More free settlers were arriving—British men and women who came to the colony of their own free will, as opposed to being sent as prisoners.

The first free settlers arrived on the *Bellona* in February 1793. They had been given free passage—as all free settlers were until 1818—as well as free land, free tools, free convict labour, and free food rations for themselves and their convicts for a year.

UP THE HAWKESBURY

Settlements were quickly spreading along the Parramatta River and up into the Hawkesbury area. Like the soil around Parramatta, the land along the Hawkesbury River was rich, and massive wheat crops could grow there with very little work.

But these were the lands of the Bidjigal people.

PROUD PEMULWUY

Pemulwuy was a young Bidjigal warrior fired by hatred and revenge. He had watched the British invade more and more Bidjigal land, transforming it into farms where the Bidjigal were no longer welcome. So he started leading attacks against the settlers. Over time, legends grew up about him, believed by both his own people and by his enemies. One legend claimed he could be in many places at once. Another said he led every attack that was made against the settlers.

Yet others declared he could not be held by chains, and that he couldn't be killed by either muskets or a white man.

BIDJIGAL BATTLES

The Bidjigal could see how fast the Eora lands had been invaded and settled by the white colonists. They didn't want the fertile lands along the Parramatta and Hawkesbury Rivers to be taken over too. Led by Pemulwuy, they began a series of raids and attacks on settlers in the area between present-day Parramatta and Toongabbie.

In February 1794 a group of Eora men in the Parramatta area badly beat some settlers' wives and took their corn. In April 1794, a dozen Eora people tried to take bags of corn from a farm at Toongabbie, but were driven away by constables. The Eora returned that night, and one of them was shot dead. His head was preserved in alcohol and sent to England to be studied and put in a museum.

By 1795 many of the Eora had died or been forced to move into other people's lands. Pemulwuy's followers came from many places, not just from amongst his own people.

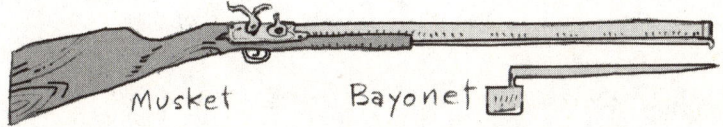

Musket   Bayonet

In October 1794 a settler called Forrester shot a Bidjigal boy as he was struggling across the Hawkesbury River with his hands bound. Forrester claimed he shot the boy to stop him getting back to his people and telling them that the settlers had only one musket between them.

In May 1795 a farmer named Wilson and his labourer, Thorp, were killed. Captain Paterson ordered soldiers to track the Bidjigal men down, kill as many as they could, then hang the bodies on gibbets as a warning to other Bidjigal. The soldiers claimed that they did shoot some Bidjigal, but that the men's bodies were carried away by fellow Bidjigal people. Then a man, five women and their children were taken prisoner. The man escaped. One of the women and her baby were shot at and pierced by the same bullet. Both eventually died.

Captain Paterson hoped that, after this, the Bidjigal would be frightened into 'behaving' themselves. The troops went back to Sydney—and Pemulwuy's men attacked again. This time they killed William Rowe and his son. They also wounded the boy's mother, who crawled bleeding to the river and hid amongst the reeds in the water until the warriors left.

In spite of the attacks, many of the Bidjigal were friendly. And even though the settlers were all scared of possible attack by the Bidjigal, most of them never experienced one. However, after these attacks troops were permanently stationed in all areas to protect the settlers.

Exploring New Holland

In October 1795 two young men with a longing for adventure - Surgeon George Bass and Midshipman Matthew Flinders - sailed the Tom Thumb to Botany Bay and up the Georges River. Then in 1796 they took a larger boat, Tom Thumb II, and with Bass's servant, William Martin, explored further south.

The sharks down here are large enough to swallow Tom Thumb whole!

One day they rowed up a stream and attempted to show the local Aboriginals how friendly they were by offering to cut their hair and beards.

August, 1796

Bass sets sail again and discovers a great seam of coal 32 km south of Botany Bay.

John Hunter.

CHAPTER 11

GOVERNOR HUNTER HAS A GO

The new governor, Captain John Hunter, arrived from England in September 1795. Governor Hunter had been one of the senior officers of the First Fleet. He had gone back to England in March 1791—some time after the wreck of his ship, the *Sirius*—where he wrote a book about his experiences at Port Jackson and Norfolk Island. Now he was back and everything had changed. The colony was in the grip of the Rum Corps. Would he be able to take back the power the Corps had stolen?

THE TRAGEDY OF BENNELONG

Governor Hunter was accompanied by Bennelong. Bennelong had been away for three years. He was homesick, ill, and tired of the cold English weather. His companion, Yemmerrawannie, had died the year before, of either tuberculosis or pneumonia, so Bennelong had been lonely too.

While Bennelong was away, his second wife had left him. He tried to get another wife, but no-one wanted him—maybe because of his violence towards women; or because he was often drunk; or because his old friends considered him to be proud and full of himself after his trip to England.

Bennelong continued to help translate and negotiate between the two cultures, but he belonged to neither. He became an alcoholic, and was loud, quarrelsome and often violent when drunk.

BENNELONG'S BEST MATE

James Squire was transported for stealing five hens and four roosters from his neighbour. He arrived on the First Fleet and in 1790 was made one of Governor Phillip's guards. When Phillip was speared at Manly, it was Squire who stayed with him and helped him to the boat. This was the strange beginning of a long friendship between Squire and Bennelong.

> Squire was the first brewer in Sydney.

Bennelong had a hut in Squire's orchard at Kissing Point, with a view across the harbour to the land of Bennelong's clan. This is where Bennelong ended his days. Some accounts say that Bennelong simply died. Others say that he was killed in a fight. Squire had Bennelong buried on his property, and later put up a plaque there for his friend.

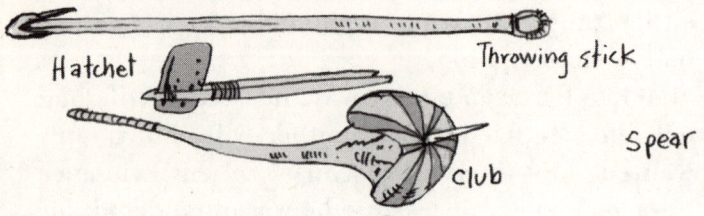

Hatchet

Throwing stick

Spear

club

HUNTER HUNTS THE CORPS

One of Governor Hunter's first acts was to give the magistrates back their powers. This meant that the free settlers could at last speak out when members of the Corps raped their wives, killed their friends, demanded their properties to pay back a debt or sold them alcohol at 1200 percent profit. Hunter also tried to stop the Corps making their own alcohol.

But the Corps was too powerful. Hardly anything could be said or done against them without them taking revenge. When a foreman dobbed in a guard who'd left his post, a gang of Corps soldiers wrecked his house. When Hunter tried to arrest the soldiers, the Corps threatened him, and he was forced to back down.

The Corps did everything they could to get rid of Governor Hunter. Lieutenant John Macarthur sent letters to the British Government saying that whatever went wrong in the colony was the governor's fault. He also claimed that Hunter let convicts do nothing while they were fed at government expense. While he was at it, Macarthur slipped in a demand that he be given another forty hectares, as well as the men needed to work on it.

A Home or a Temporary Prison?

Despite the fertile soil and the wonderful climate, most of the new settlers intended to return to Britain once they had made their fortunes—or, if they were convicts, at the end of their sentences.

Even the British Government didn't think that the colony would last forever. In June 1798 the British Government worked out that it would actually be much cheaper to keep the convicts in England. Britain simply wasn't getting much in return for all it had spent. The colony had been going for ten years and it still needed outside help to survive. Would it survive if Britain stopped sending convicts?

Exploring New Holland
September, 1797

LIEUTENANT JOHN SHORTLAND GOES NORTH.

He fails to find the escaped convicts.

"Can't see them."

But he discovers seams of coal...

"Hang on! Is this what I think it is?"

...and a great river that he calls the Hunter, after his governor.

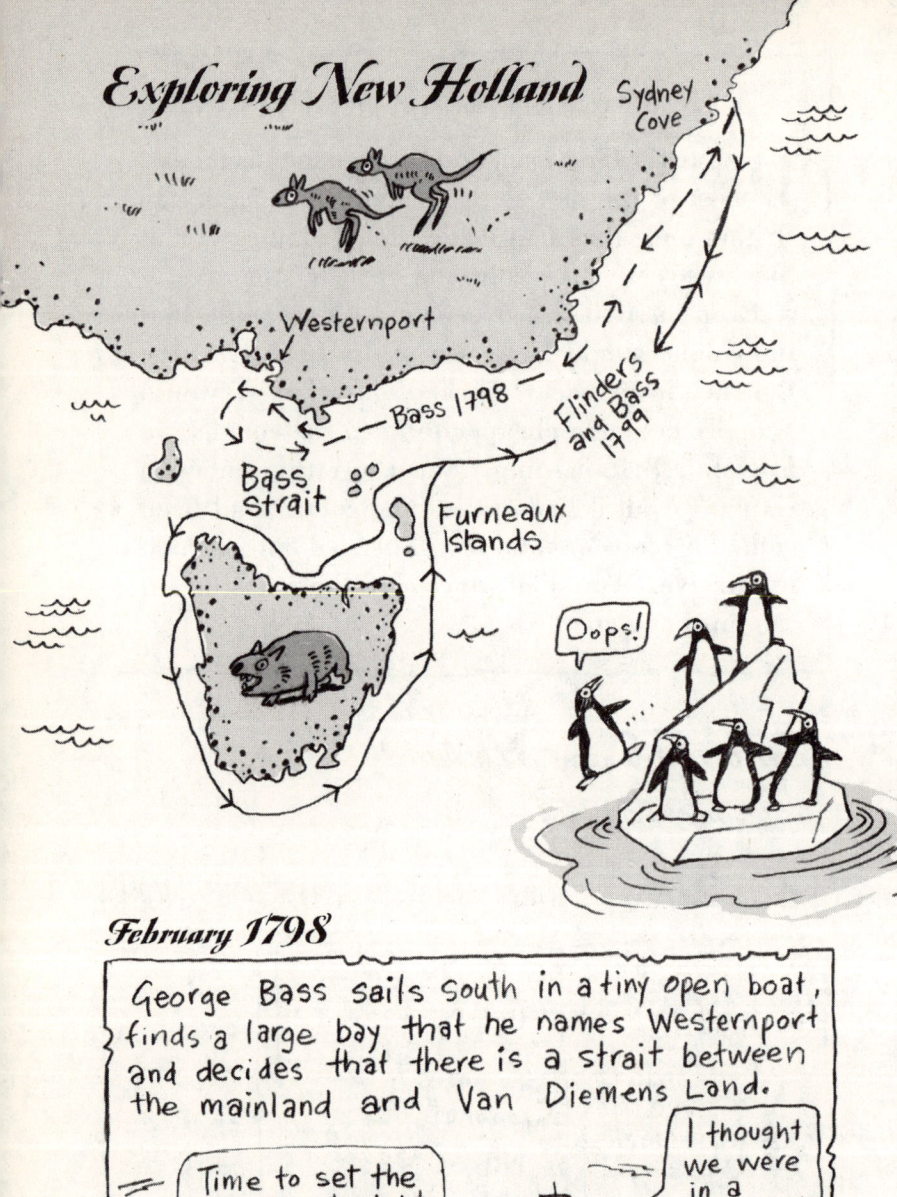

Exploring New Holland

Sydney Cove

Westernport

Flinders and Bass 1799

— Bass 1798 —

Bass Strait

Furneaux Islands

Oops!

February 1798

George Bass sails south in a tiny open boat, finds a large bay that he names Westernport and decides that there is a strait between the mainland and Van Diemens Land.

Time to set the record straight. We are in a strait.

I thought we were in a whaleboat.

March 1798

John Wilson was a convict on the First Fleet. When his time expired he lived in the bush and was called 'the wild white man'. He explored the country south of Sydney and brought back a lyrebird to Sydney Cove.

Because you have a tail like Apollo's lyre you shall be called a Lyrebird.

How much can a koala bear?

March 1798

Matthew Flinders sails south to the newly named Bass Strait and he too confirms that it is a strait. He sees a strange animal on one of the Furneaux Islands. The local people call it a Wom Bat.

They are hilarious when they are alive.

October 1798–January 1799

Bass and Flinders sail around Van Diemen's Land and chart many of the Bass Strait islands.

Your turn to row, Bass.

Straight!

THE RUM CORPS STILL RULES!

In June 1798 Governor Hunter made a rule that anyone—and not just members of the Corps—should be allowed to buy goods from visiting ships. But the New South Wales Corps officers didn't like this at all. They formed a group which would stop anyone else from muscling in on their trade.

By this time even people in Britain were gossiping about the scandals in New South Wales—such as Rum Corps officers choosing convict women like cattle as soon as transports came into harbour; or borrowing their future pay from the regiment's funds to spend on goods; or forcing small farmers to sell them their farms. When Governor Hunter received a petition signed by eighteen settlers who wanted to buy tools directly from visiting ships, the Corps ignored both the petition and the governor.

The Home Secretary ordered Governor Hunter to conduct an inquiry into the bad behaviour of the officers. But how could Governor Hunter do anything? The people who were supposed to enforce the law were the very ones who were breaking it.

The colony's first theatre was opened in 1796. It had to be closed again in 1798 because so many houses were burgled while their owners were watching the shows!

NICE PUSSYCAT!

Flogging was a cheap form of punishment. Anyone could be flogged—men, women and even children. Major crimes like murder were punished by hanging. Most thefts were punished by adding an extra seven years to someone's sentence. Really big thefts and rape were punished with hard labour or work in a chain gang. For anything else, there was flogging. About forty percent of prisoners were flogged at some time.

Most prisoners were flogged with the cat-o'-nine-tails, with its nine separate lashes.

space required to swing a cat-o'-nine-tails.

Space required to swing a cat.

A flogger could decide to whip lightly, or else so hard that the whip cut into the flesh. Some whips had knots at the end of each lash that ripped into the skin.

Sometimes all the lashes were given in a single flogging. Two hundred lashes would leave a person scarred for life, and they would spend months recovering. Five hundred lashes all at once was as good as a death sentence—after that many lashes in a single dose, most died in agony, infection or heart failure.

But the punishment was often spread over days or even months, so that there was time to recover between each whipping. If you were lucky, a bucket of salt water would be thrown over your back after your flogging. This stung, and many people passed out with the pain—but the salt cleaned the wounds. If you were really lucky, you would get maggots in your wounds. The maggots ate the dead flesh and stopped your back from rotting.

Some typical sentences were:
- stealing a pair of shoes—25 lashes
- being rude to your master—50 lashes
- sending a signal to your mates that the overseer was coming so they'd better get back to work—25 lashes
- throwing stones at an overseer—30 lashes
- swearing at the overseer—50 lashes
- drunkenness and stealing alcohol—50 lashes
- not doing the job you'd been told to do—150 lashes
- telling lies about the overseer—150 lashes
- taking a day off without permission—150 lashes

SAVAGE SEALERS

The colony's third settlement was on Cape Barren Island in Bass Strait. Sealers set up camp there in 1798, building huts, a processing plant and establishing a vegetable garden. The seals showed no fear of humans—and nine thousand were clubbed to death in two months. Seals, especially baby seals, were valuable for their waterproof skins. Seal oil was used for lamps, cooking oil, for lubricating machinery, for making soap and processing jute, and as a leather dressing. In 1802, 25 600 seal furs and tonnes of seal oil were shipped to China from the Bass Strait Islands.

The seals still showed no fear of humans. One sealer even had a giant pet elephant seal that came when he called and let him ride on its back.

FLOOD WARNING

In late February 1799 settlers along the Hawkesbury were puzzled by some unusual behaviour from the Bidjigal people, who were yelling and making strange gestures. The settlers and the Bidjigal were almost in a state of war—so what could all this mean?

On March 3 the settlers found out. Wild floodwaters turned farmland along the river into an inland sea. Only a few roofs and hilltops remained visible above the swirling water. One man drowned, and many had to be rescued by boat. Some settlers had to fire their muskets into the air to let rescuers know where they were.

Despite the bad relations between settlers and Indigenous people, the Bidjigal had been trying to warn the settlers of the coming floods.

CONFUSION IN COURT

In 1799 five white settlers killed two Aboriginals. They were tried and found guilty of murder. Many settlers thought this was unfair, but Governor Hunter insisted that, according to the laws set down by Governor Phillip, the Aboriginal people were subjects of the King and anyone who killed them was guilty of murder. But the court couldn't work out how to punish the murderers, so they were released.

MY TICKET OUTTA HERE!

Many convicts escaped the colony by signing up as crew on visiting ships. Ships were often short of crew because ship life was hard, dangerous and dirty; the food was terrible; and many sailors died. Ships' captains welcomed the escaping convicts and would hide them until the ship left port.

Exploring New Holland

July–August 1799

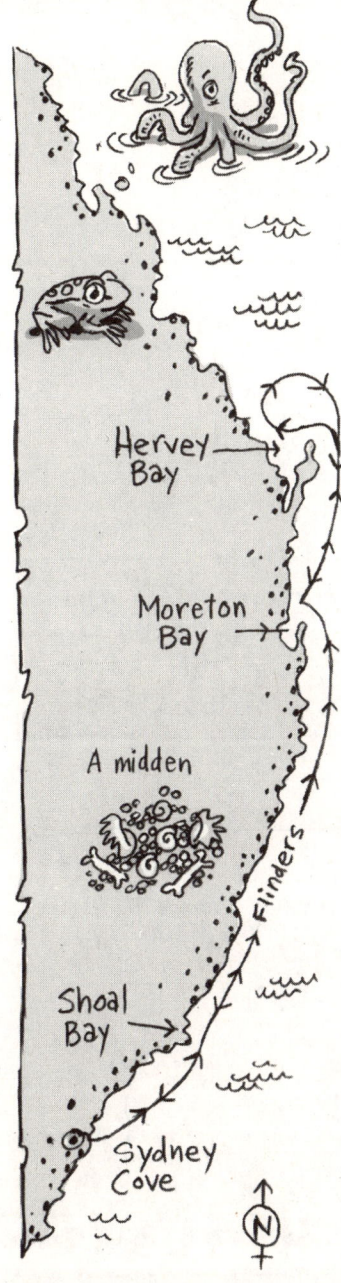

Flinders sailed north from the Sydney settlement looking for large rivers that he could sail up. He found no river at Shoal Bay, but he did find a number of Aboriginal dwellings. These houses were far more solid than the huts that the white settlers had so far seen, and were made of woven vines with bark cladding.

Flinders decided that although Moreton Bay was pretty, its harbour was too shallow. He then sailed north to Hervey Bay, which he decided was too exposed. In those days all new settlements depended on good harbours.

Matthew Flinders.

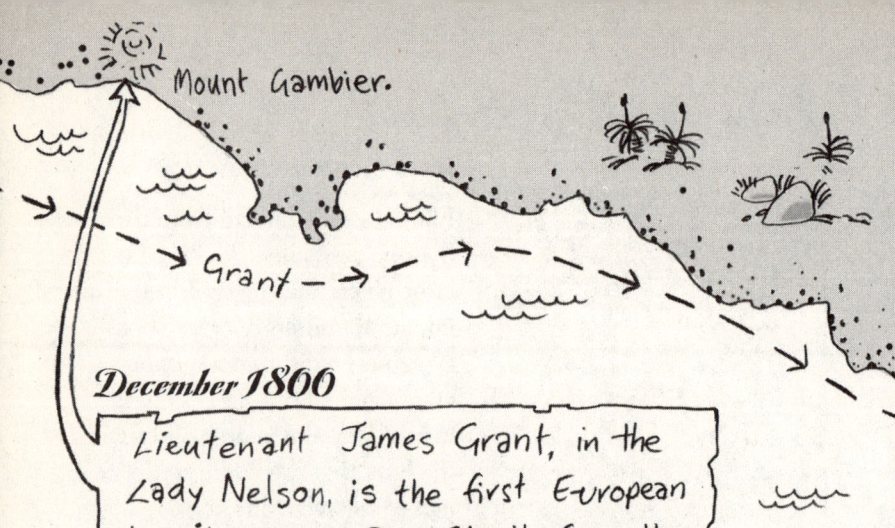

Mount Gambier.

Grant →

December 1806

Lieutenant James Grant, in the Lady Nelson, is the first European to sail through Bass Strait from the west. He names Mount Gambier.

March–May 1801

Grant then sails into Westernport and, after exploring the country, he builds a blockhouse and plants a fruit and vegetable garden on Churchill Island.

September 1801

Local Aboriginals at Westernport demand that the British, under the command of Lieutenant John Murray, take off their clothes before they will talk to them.

> OK, fatso, let's talk.

Port Phillip Bay

Westernport.

Churchill Island.

Grant

Murray

Murray

to Sydney

King Is.

January, February and March 1802

Murray tries to enter Port Phillip Bay but is held back twice by bad weather. When he finally enters the bay the local Aboriginals try to make him leave. Murray initially calls the bay Port King but King himself later decides it should be called Port Phillip.

Get lost!

Philip Gidley King

CHAPTER 12

GOVERNOR KING TAKES THE REINS

The old and sickly Governor Hunter left for England in September 1800. He was worn out from trying to reform a colony of crooks. The new governor, Philip Gidley King, had been the commander at Norfolk Island. He was an able and intelligent naval officer. But would that be enough to defeat the Corps?

The colony was still controlled by the Rum Corps. Rum was the colony's money, and also an escape from all sorts of things, from bad weather to boredom. Many convicts were almost permanently drunk—so drunk that they didn't bother to harvest the crops on their small pieces of land, even if they were starving. Orphans roamed the streets of Sydney Town, abandoned by drunken parents.

King immediately decided to act tough. He forbade masters to flog their convict servants without permission from a magistrate. He refused to let two American ships unload their cargoes of alcohol. From now on, he said, only small amounts could be landed and bought for private use, but not the enormous quantities bought by the Corps. Convicts who had won a ticket-of-leave were no longer supported by government rations, but had to either work for themselves, or get a job.

SHOOTING THE BOSS

In September 1801 Lieutenant-Colonel William Paterson showed John Macarthur a letter he'd written to Sir Joseph Banks criticising Governor King. Macarthur went straight to King and told him about it. Paterson was furious with Macarthur for dobbing him in, and challenged Macarthur to a duel. Paterson was Macarthur's commanding officer, but Macarthur shot him in the shoulder with a pistol and won the duel.

King arrested Macarthur then offered to release him again until his court martial. Macarthur refused to be released until he had a written statement of the charges against him. Finally, King sent him off to England to face court martial there, hoping that this would get rid of him. (Strangely, incriminating records that were sent along with Macarthur mysteriously disappeared on the journey!)

But Macarthur would return!

> A court martial is a trial held by the military to judge military men.

Exploring New Holland

April–September 1801

Two French ships, Le *Géographe* and Le *Naturaliste*, led by Captain Nicolas Baudin, and with the cartographer and surveyor Louis Claude Freycinet, mapped the west coast of New Holland.

Investigator

July 1801

Flinders sailed from England in a rotting boat, the *Investigator*. It was too leaky to use to fight the French, but Flinders hoped to use it to chart the coast of New Holland. He reached Cape Leeuwin in December.

December 1801–May 1802

Flinders started charting the south coast of New Holland. Seven of his crew were killed when the boat crashed on the rocks at Cape Catastrophe, and Flinders named the islands in the area after his lost seamen.

He also named Kangaroo Island, after the large numbers of kangaroos he saw there. These kangaroos had no fear of humans, and came up close to the explorers—so the sailors shot and ate the trusting animals, and the men made caps out of the skins.

In April Flinders and Baudin met at Encounter Bay. Baudin was scornful of the chart of Bass Strait that Flinders was using, until he discovered (to his amazement) that the chart had been made in an open boat. He was even more amazed the next morning when he realised he was talking to the guy who made the map!

Flinders arrived in Sydney in May 1802 and, after refitting the ship, continued sailing north in July. Despite his ship falling

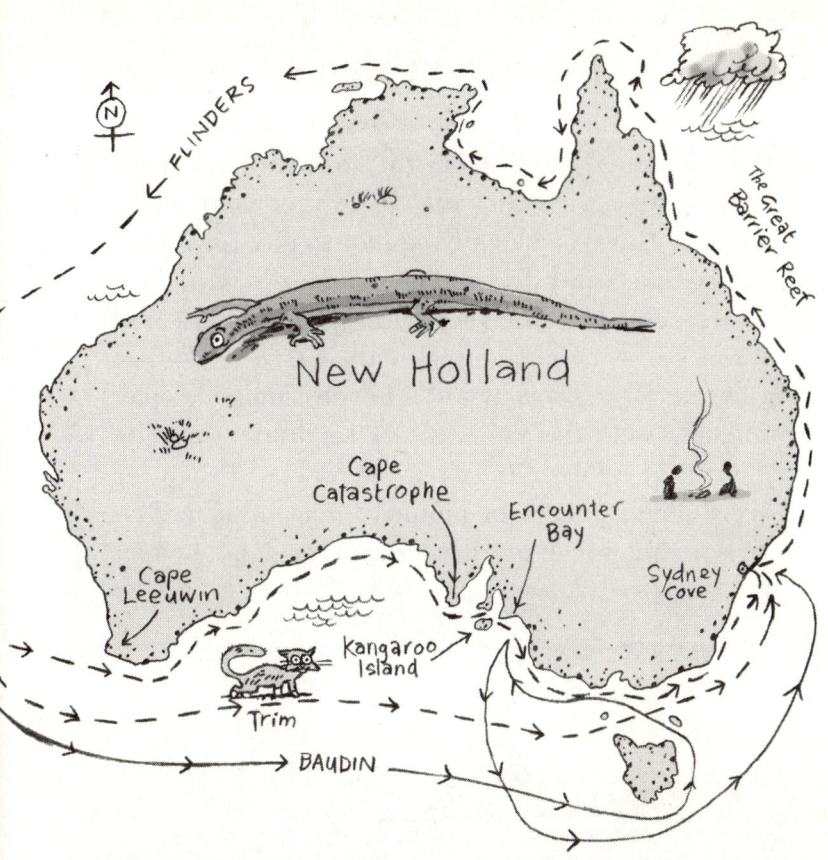

to bits, and despite monsoons, and the dangerous rocks of the Great Barrier Reef, Flinders decided to try and press on up the east coast of New Holland and circumnavigate the continent.

July 1803

After sailing around the entire coastline of New Holland, Flinders sailed back into Sydney in July 1803, more than two years after setting out. He had survived crippling scurvy from the lack of fresh food, the loss of seven of his crew from illness, and another seven from shipwreck and battles with local people. His rotting ship was immediately declared unseaworthy. But Flinders had finally sailed around the coastline of New Holland.

Expensive Sydney!

Governor and Mrs King received free salt pork, wheat and sugar from the government stores, and vegies and fruit from the government house garden. But Governor King had to pay for all his other food—and it was expensive!

By 1800 most of the Rum Corp officers had farms and convicts, and grew their own food—but Governor King's salary was hardly enough to pay for mutton at five shillings per kg, butter (usually rancid) at eight shillings per kg, a cake of soap for six shillings and eight pounds for a kg of tea! (A reasonable wage in those days was about sixty pounds a year.)

RUFFIANS IN THE ROCKS

By 1803 you could eat out at The Rocks in Sydney Town. But only if you were brave enough. Rosetta Stabler served boiled mutton and broths every day at midday, and roast meat at 1.00 pm. But The Rocks was filled with cutthroats and pickpockets. There were also 'crimping gangs', who would bash you up or drug your drink, steal your purse, and then sell you to a captain who needed crew for his ship!

Death of Pemulwuy

In June 1802 Pemulwuy, along with another of his men, was finally shot by two settlers. Pemulwuy lay on the ground with four musket balls in his body. Could the invincible Pemulwuy survive even this? After all, legend had it that Pemulwuy could not be killed by either a musket or a white man. So, to make sure he died, Pemulwuy's head was cut from his body with a sword. The invincible man of power was no more.

Some Bidjigal people offered Pemulwuy's head to Governor King as a way of showing they wanted peace. Governor King had the head put in a jar of alcohol and sent it to Sir Joseph Banks in England. King also sent a letter describing Pemulwuy as a 'terrible pest'. However, King admitted that Pemulwuy had also been brave and independent.

Aboriginal people had been forbidden to go near Parramatta, but in return for the friendly gift of Pemulwuy's head, Governor King gave orders that they should be allowed to return, and that no-one was to hurt them. And for a while it looked like the Parramatta-Hawkesbury war might end.

But the killings continued.

John Llewellyn, a military settler, was eating lunch with a workman when he invited an Aboriginal known as Branch Jack to join them. Branch Jack grabbed Llewellyn's musket as twenty other Bidjigal men launched an attack with spears and axes. They killed Llewellyn and left the workman close to death. Then they burnt a nearby house, killing two more settlers.

King sent troops to guard the outlying settlements. He forbade any Aboriginal person to approach settlers' houses. The highest ranking judge in the colony decided that Aboriginal people shouldn't be allowed to stand trial for their crimes. For a start, he said, Aboriginal people couldn't 'swear by God' to tell the truth, as they didn't have a religion (or so he thought). They didn't know how to plead 'guilty' or 'not guilty'.

This meant that Aboriginal people could be pursued, punished and even killed without ever having the opportunity to tell their side of the story.

On the Sheep's Back

In the early days of the colony sheep were valued for their meat, not their wool. In 1797 Captain Henry Waterhouse was the first to bring merino sheep to New South Wales. The Reverend Samuel Marsden, John Macarthur and other Rum Corps officers bought these merinos to breed. Governor King was so impressed by their fine wool that he sent some to Sir Joseph Banks.

War with France meant that English cloth manufacturers could no longer buy fine fleece from Saxony and Spain. When Macarthur arrived in England for his court martial, the cloth manufacturers approached him with a plan. Could they buy merino wool from New South Wales instead? The British Government even gave Macarthur an additional two thousand hectares for grazing sheep. Macarthur suddenly discovered that there was money to be made in wool.

Macarthur, counting woolly jumpers.

Meanwhile, back in the colony, the Reverend Samuel Marsden had been improving sheep breeds. Marsden was known as the best farmer in the colony and, in 1807, he was the first to sell wool to England. Marsden would have been called *The Father of the Wool Industry*—if John Macarthur hadn't rewritten history to keep that title for himself.

MARVELLOUS MRS MACARTHUR

Elizabeth Macarthur accompanied her husband, John Macarthur, to Port Jackson in 1790. Some say she was the first educated woman to arrive in Australia; and she was the only woman to be invited to dine with Governor Phillip.

Elizabeth Macarthur.

Visitors had to bring their own bread when they dined with the governor, but there was always a bread roll at the governor's table for Mrs Macarthur.

When Governor Phillip left the colony, Major Francis Grose gave John Macarthur forty hectares at Parramatta, which the Macarthurs called Elizabeth Farm. Desperate to encourage the officers to take farming seriously, Major Grose also offered forty hectares to the first officer who could turn twenty hectares into farmland.

In the days when ladies spent their time gossiping, embroidering and drinking tea, Elizabeth soon discovered that she had an unsuspected genius—for farming. Elizabeth and John won the contest easily. By 1794 Elizabeth Farm had forty hectares of productive farmland, another thirty hectares ready to be planted with potatoes and maize, and two thousand bushels of wheat in store.

The wheat crop alone was enough to a make the Macarthurs rich. But they also had a thriving orchard, vineyard, hen runs, vegetable gardens and half a dozen greyhounds for hunting wild duck and kangaroos.

It was Elizabeth who ran the farm during her husband's two absences. While John was in England between 1801 and 1805, she was the first in the colony to sell hay; she grew twenty-two kinds of fruit. In fact, she grew so much fruit that she fed her pigs on spoiled apricots, melons and peaches to get rid of it all.

When John was later exiled between 1808 and 1817, Elizabeth ran their new two-thousand-hectare grant at Camden Park. She coped with frost, drought, floods and attacks by the Bidjigal people. Her main interest was improving and producing the wool of the merino sheep. When her husband asked her to join him in England, Elizabeth refused: she wanted to stay and develop her farms. As well as being a farmer, Elizabeth bore and raised nine children, some of whom became famous politicians or farming pioneers.

When John Macarthur died insane in 1834, Elizabeth continued to run the family businesses for another sixteen years.

'THE FLOGGING PARSON'

Samuel Marsden arrived in the colony in 1794. After the Reverend Richard Johnson left in 1800, Marsden became the senior Church of England minister. He was a devoted clergyman, but he was often cruel to his family and servants, as well as intolerant towards wrongdoers. He ordered flogging for the smallest offences—such as being rude to your master.

Marsden refused to work with emancipists, as he didn't believe an ex-convict could be his equal; and he was disgusted by convict women, Catholics, and Aboriginals who refused to convert to Christianity.

As well as working hard for the Church, Marsden became one of the colony's leading graziers.

Exploring New Holland

December 1862

Ensign Francis Barrallier, a Frenchman serving in the NSW Corps, travelled 225kms into the Jenolan Caves area of the Blue Mountains.

But, like others before him, he was forced to turn back by unscaleable waterfalls...

...all the while hearing the coo-ee of the local Aboriginal people, who had long had their own paths through the mountains.

THE GREAT INLAND SEA

In many countries big rivers either begin or end in great lakes. New Holland had big rivers, so the logic went that somewhere there must also be a giant inland sea. Many rivers also seemed to run inland, which supported this theory. Some thought this sea might start at Spencer Gulf, and that perhaps the whole of inland Australia was lush green grass. Flinders proved that there was no opening at Spencer Gulf to an inland sea. But many explorers still dreamt that they'd discover this sea over the next hill.

September 1803

Flinders attempts to sail back to England aboard the Porpoise, carrying maps of New Holland.

The Cato and Bridgewater sail at the same time. The Cato and Porpoise are wrecked on Wreck Reef 1200 km north of Sydney.

The Bridgewater ignores the disaster and keeps sailing north.

Flinders survives with others by struggling to a sandbank. But they still need to be rescued.

Flinders returns to Sydney by sailing 13 days in a small cutter.

In Sydney.

I need a new ship.

He then sets out again in the small, old and rotting ship, the Cumberland.

He rescues everyone left on the sandbank.

Hooray!

Sails the Cumberland to French controlled Ile de France (now called Mauritius)

Africa

Madagascar

N

Bonjour.

But as soon as he arrives he is arrested as a spy.

Pourquoi?

Unknown to Flinders, England and France are again at war.

So Flinders sends his charts of New Holland to Sir Joseph Banks in England.

To Joe

He is not released till 1810.

Ho hum.

FEARLESS MATTHEW FLINDERS

Flinders joined the navy at fifteen. He arrived in Port Jackson as a master's mate on the *Reliance* with his friend George Bass, the ship's surgeon. After his extraordinary achievements in the colony and his final release from Ile de France, Flinders sailed back to England and his wife, where he published *A Voyage to Terra Australis*. In this book he suggested that the continent of New Holland should be known as *Australia*. The name caught on. He died the day after he saw his book in print.

Nicolas Baudin

CHAPTER 13

VAN DIEMEN'S LAND

New South Wales was settled by the British partly to keep the French from grabbing it first. But one small colony in Port Jackson couldn't protect the whole of a huge continent.

French ships were still surveying the coast, studying the plants and animals and Indigenous people. Governor King welcomed Captain Baudin and the French ships when they visited Sydney in 1802, but when he looked at their maps and saw that they had given French names to a British possession, he began to get worried! As soon as the French ships left, Governor King sent Lieutenant Charles Robbins to follow them. Robbins caught up with them on King Island in Bass Strait.

THE FLAG FIASCO

Robbins found the French quietly studying wildlife and plants. But he had his orders. So on 14 December 1802 Robbins raised the Union Jack, fired a volley and proclaimed the island a British possession. Unfortunately, he raised the flag upside-down! The French were not impressed. Baudin wrote to Governor King and told him that the whole thing was childish—and that the upside-down flag was not at all majestic!

FRENCH INVASION?

Baudin was supposed to be mapping the coast, but according to the diaries of his deputy captain, Francois Péron, Le *Naturaliste* was really a spy ship for Napoleon! Napoleon's plan had been to invade New South Wales, and he hoped that the rebel Irish convicts in the colony would turn against the British colony and assist the French. But Baudin and Peron didn't think much of the Irish convicts, and the invasion never happened.

Instead of sailing below Van Diemen's Land into the storms, British ships now were sailing through Bass Strait to get back to England. This cut about two weeks off the journey. But if the French decided to settle on either side of Bass Strait, they might stop the British from using it.

Governor King decided it was time to make it clear who owned Van Diemen's Land. Not the French. Not the American whaling captains who hunted the rich whaling grounds near the Derwent River. And certainly not the people who had already been living there for thousands of years.

Governor Phillip had claimed Van Diemen's land in 1788, so it was already British. But the only way to *keep* it British was to start more colonies.

FLIES AND LOBSTERS AT PORT PHILLIP

In October 1803 Lieutenant-Colonel David Collins was sent from England to Sullivan Bay in Port Phillip. His job was to create a settlement there. Governor King also began plans for a settlement in Van Diemen's Land so that the British could control both side of Bass Strait.

Sullivan Bay was supposed to have great soil and good water. But when the settlers arrived after their long voyage from England, they found sand dunes, hordes of biting flies and temperatures over 40°C. There was little fresh water or game. They had to live on lobsters, and they were hot, thirsty, and became increasingly ill in their canvas town.

Worse still, it looked as though they would have to fight if they wanted to claim the land. Not with the French, but with the local Boonwurrung people. Collins wrote to Governor King saying that he would need four times as many soldiers, as the upper part of the harbour was 'full of natives'—and they were not friendly.

Perhaps news of the eight-year struggle between black and white in the Parramatta and Hawkesbury districts had been passed along Aboriginal trade routes. Perhaps Collins didn't know how to show the local people that he wanted to be friends. Or perhaps the Boonwurrung simply didn't want newcomers taking over their land.

The new settlers fired on the local inhabitants, killing one, wounding others, and burning a hut. Their plan was to show them the deadly effects of their firearms, but it didn't really work, as the danger continued.

Did you know that the early Hobart settlers ate crap? Crap was the burnt blubber that was dumped from American whaling ships. The settlers found it washed up on the beaches.

THE FOUNDING OF HOBART TOWN

On 13 September 1803 Lieutenant John Bowen set up camp at Risdon Cove on the Derwent River in Van Diemen's Land. He had forty-nine people with him, including twenty-four convicts, some free settlers and some soldiers of the New South Wales Corps. They named their new settlement after Lord Hobart, who was in charge of the colonies in the British Government.

This settlement seemed promising. The countryside looked like an English park, with fertile soil, green grass and scattered giant trees. Better still, after an initial meeting when Bowen first arrived, the local Mouheneer people had not been seen.

PORT PHILLIP ABANDONED

Collins soon realised that Port Phillip Bay was no place for a town. So King told Collins to set up a colony in Van Diemen's Land, either in the north, or with Bowen in the south. But when he tried the north, his men were too sick to do anything, and the local inhabitants looked just as warlike as the Boonwurrung had. So he decided to keep sailing and join up with Hobart Town. He landed his 260 people, including 178 convicts, across the river from Risdon Cove, at a better place where there was an excellent site for landing. Bowen and his settlers soon crossed the river to join Collins, who was now in charge.

Like the other settlements, Hobart Town had problems from the beginning. There were too many convicts and too few free settlers. There were also too few guards, because many soldiers had refused to go to Van Diemen's Land at all. Cold winds battered the ragged tents, and the new settlement was so desperately short of food that they lived on kangaroo and boiled seaweed. But despite these hardships, the fertile river flats were planted with crops and the free settlers were given farms.

The colonists' dogs also hunted down a strange animal that looked like a wolf or a hyena. The first Tasmanian tiger had been killed by white settlement.

The People of Van Diemen's Land

It is difficult to know exactly where people lived in Tasmania before white settlers arrived, because so many were killed before maps had been drawn. But this is pretty close.

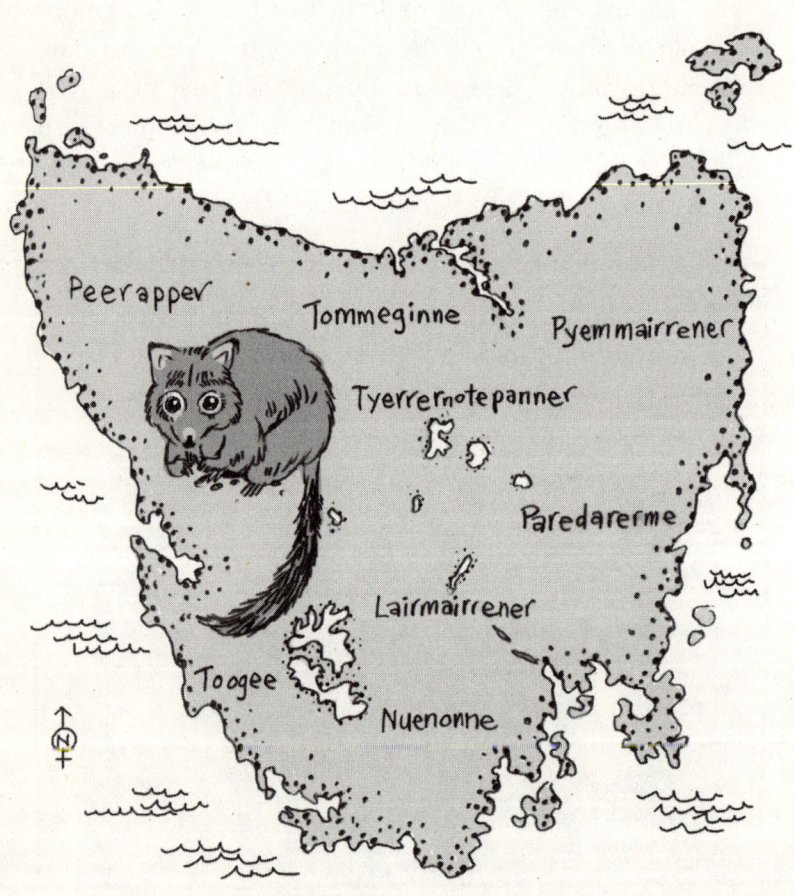

THE LOOMING TRAGEDY

The people of Hobart Town continually feared attack from the Mouheneer (one of the groups in the south-east). After all, attacks were still going on in the Sydney region, and the Port Phillip settlement had been abandoned partly because of the warlike people there. .

I'll shoot the next evil monster who calls me paranoid.

This fear was soon to lead to tragedy. In May 1804 several hundred armed Mouheneer men headed toward the settlement. They were probably just on a kangaroo hunt, but to the nervous soldiers they must have looked terrifying. The soldiers opened fire with muskets and cannon and killed about forty men.

Of the three to eight thousand Aboriginal people in Van Diemen's Land when the Europeans arrived, there were only about one thousand left seventeen years later. Most of them were killed by disease brought by the settlers. During that same period, only five Europeans were killed by Aboriginals. (This was far fewer than the number killed by bushrangers, who were the settlers' own countrymen.)

What's in a Name?

On 4 November 1804 a settlement was started on the Tamar River in the north of Van Diemen's Land. The landing place at the mouth of the river had been named Port Dalrymple by Bass and Flinders in 1798. In 1804 Paterson and his party set up a camp where George Town (named after King George III) now stands. A few weeks later the settlement was moved across the river to York Town (named after the Duke of York), and a year later was finally settled in Launceston (which was briefly known as Patersonia). Launceston was named to honour Governor King who came from Launceston in Cornwall, England.

Most early Australian towns, rivers and bays were named after Englishmen. These men have now mostly been forgotten, but they live on as placenames in a land some of them never saw!

HUNGRY HOBART

Hobart Town grew hungrier and no ships came. It was like the Sydney Cove settlement all over again. There was no tea, no sugar and no vegetables—except wild greens.

In the harsh cold winter of 1805 Collins reduced the flour ration to one kilogram a week. Even so, that only left them with supplies for six weeks. Then, early in October, two ships sailed up the river. But instead of bringing supplies, the ships were in desperate need of food themselves. Nine men on one of the ships were dying of starvation!

The following year was worse—but no grain ships came from Sydney. By September 1806 there was no flour at all, and no tea, sugar or wine. Even the previous summer's vegetables had all been eaten.

In desperation, Collins turned the convicts out into the bush with muskets to hunt kangaroos and birds. Unfortunately, many of those convicts were never seen again. Nor were the muskets! The convicts ran away to become 'bolters'.

BOLTING BUSHRANGERS!

The first bushrangers weren't crooks. The word 'bushranger' was used to describe anyone who was an expert in bushcraft! But convict bush experts often became 'bolters' and survived by terrorising and stealing from settlers. By 1805 'bushranger' already referred to a thief who lived in the bush and stole to survive.

At last, in October 1806, the *Royal George* arrived with supplies from England. More food arrived from England early the following year. Things began to look brighter. The colony now had enough food to survive—but only just— and it had a new whaling industry that brought in money.

A whaling station had been built at Ralph's Bay. The bay was so thick with dead whales that boats had to keep close to shore to avoid running into them. Nearly three hundred men worked at whaling, sealing, fishing and boiling down whale oil.

But there still weren't enough convicts and settlers for the colony to thrive. Too many convicts had escaped to the bush. And the bushranger threat was growing.

Reverend Richard Johnson.

CHAPTER 14

THE BATTLE OF VINEGAR HILL

The first convicts sent to the colony were mostly thieves. But by the mid-1790s a new sort of convict started arriving. These people were Irish political prisoners transported for rebellion.

The Irish rebels were Catholics. They wanted Ireland to be free of English rule. They wanted to be allowed to vote. And they wanted to be free to worship as Roman Catholics. Catholics in Ireland weren't allowed to own land or even go to school. In those days, people believed that you had to follow the same religion as the king. If you didn't, you weren't loyal to the king—and if you weren't loyal, you were obviously a criminal.

In the colony of New South Wales it was actually illegal to celebrate mass. All convicts had to go to the long and boring Anglican sermons of the Reverend Richard Johnson, who spent Sunday mornings trying to tell his congregation not to swear or get drunk.

In 1796 Governor Hunter complained to Britain about the number of Irish convicts that were arriving. He demanded that more English thieves be sent to balance the numbers. But after the Irish uprisings in 1796 and 1798, more Irish rebels than ever were sent to New South Wales.

Pikes and Plots

In August 1800 there were whispers about a possible Irish rebellion in the colony. Rumours had it that an uprising was planned for the end of September, and that Irish convicts had been hiding pikes. Every house in the colony was searched—except, of course, for the houses of the Rum Corps. Five Irish prisoners were sentenced to five hundred lashes each, and four to one hundred lashes. The plan was to torture them into confessing where the weapons were hidden.

> A pike is a long wooden shaft with a pointed steel or iron head.

These floggings were the most brutal ever seen in the colony. One man's bones showed through his flesh. Another man's back was turned to jelly. But none of the men admitted anything, and the pikes—if they existed—were never found.

By 1801 there were six hundred United Irish convicts in New South Wales, 135 of them desperate characters from County Cork. Some of the Irish convicts refused to work or follow orders. Others escaped and became bushrangers.

In 1803 Governor King finally allowed Roman Catholics to attend their own church services. King hoped that this would calm the Irish. But it didn't. By 1804 there were twelve hundred Irish political prisoners—in a colony of just over eight thousand people.

And now the rumours of rebellion were true.

REBELLION!

The password was 'St Peter'.

The convicts who worked at Castle Hill planned to march to the Hawkesbury area. They would join up with the convicts there, then march with more than a thousand men to seize Parramatta and set up a Liberty Pole outside Government House. The rebels then planned to march to Sydney Town, seize all the ships in the harbour and sail back to Ireland.

But the rebels were betrayed. On 3 March a convict told the commandant at Parramatta that the rebellion was planned for Sunday 4 March. Governor King heard about this, but he took no notice of the warning. There had been rumours before. Surely this was just another one.

But it wasn't.

As planned, the two hundred rebels assembled on Sunday morning at Castle Hill, under the command of 'General' Philip Cunningham. They rang a bell to sound the rebellion, set a house on fire, gave the chief flogger a taste of his own whip and seized all the weapons they could find—a few muskets, but mostly picks. Then they began their march to Parramatta.

The news of the rebellion reached Sydney by midnight. The troops of the New South Wales Corps were called out, and 150 armed men from the navy ship *Calcutta* joined them. Women and children fled from Parramatta to Sydney and gathered at the docks in case the colony was taken over by the Irish and they had to flee.

Major George Johnston, second-in-command of the Corps, took a small force to Parramatta. At dawn on Monday he learnt that the rebels had massed on a hill at Rouse Hill. The rebels' numbers were growing all the time. Soon they would be unbeatable.

The Irish rebels called their hill *Vinegar Hill* after a battle that the rebels had fought against the British in Ireland.

It's a bitter hill.

Johnston sent a trooper, and then a priest, to negotiate with the rebels. The rebels sent them back, minus the flints for the trooper's pistols. Major Johnston then rode up to the rebels himself, with a trooper holding up a white flag of truce. Rebels Philip Cunningham and William Johnston came to meet them with their swords drawn.

Major Johnston asked Cunningham what he wanted.

'Death or liberty!' Cunningham replied. 'And a ship to take us home!'

Then Major Johnston put his pistol to William Johnston's head. The trooper who was with him did the same to Cunningham. Cunningham couldn't have liberty, but Major Johnston could offer him death. Major Johnstone ordered his men, who had just appeared over the rise, to open fire on the rebel army, and then to charge with swords and fixed bayonets.

There were 223 rebels against only twenty-nine soldiers, a trooper and about fifty volunteers. The rebels should have won, especially as most of the soldiers had no experience of battle. But the rebels had few weapons and no leader. The battle lasted less than half an hour before the rebels fled, with the soldiers after them, leaving at least fifteen dead and many wounded.

In the distraction of all the firing, William Johnston escaped and fled into the bush. Cunningham was not so lucky. He was struck by a sword and left for dead as the soldiers rounded up the rebels. But Cunningham miraculously survived. He was picked up by soldiers the next day, and was hanged from the staircase outside the public store at Green Hills (later Windsor). This was where convicts picked up their rations, and Cunningham's body was left there as a warning to any other convict who might dream of rebelling.

The rebels were rounded up and either flogged or imprisoned. Several were murdered by the soldiers. Other suspects were taken from their farms and Governor King made Catholic mass illegal again.

The rebellion was over.

HERO OR CHEAT?

Raising a white flag of truce means that you aren't going to fight. Truces are for rescuing your dead and wounded from the battlefield, or for discussing peace. But Major Johnston used the white flag of truce to trick the rebels. Was he a cheat or a hero?

We will never know the full story of the Vinegar Hill rebellion. It frightened the government so badly that it erased almost all record of it. The government even refused to put Vinegar Hill on any map. We are not even sure exactly which hill it was. There are many slightly different versions of the story. What we know is mostly from people like Elizabeth Macarthur, who mentioned the rebellion in their letters, but who may not have known the whole truth.

Newcastle was established in 1804 as a prison for dangerous convicts. Many of the Castle Hill rebels were sent there after the rebellion to work in the coal mines.

HARD YAKKA

How much land should I clear in my seven years?

Convicts were supposed to work ten hours a day, Monday to Friday, and six hours on Saturdays. But as there were very few supervisors to make sure they kept working, they were often set tasks instead. For example, clearing half a hectare of land was considered one week's work.

In the early famine years convicts were let off work at three o'clock so they could tend their own gardens. This became the custom, and convicts who worked after that were paid for the extra hours. As there was so little money in the colony they were sometimes paid in wheat, but more often in rum.

COUNTING THE MOB

Of seven thousand white people in New South Wales in 1805, 3863 were men, 1370 were women and 1747 were children. Of these, 2077 were convicts; 641 were military; 617 were free settlers, 916 were freed convict men and 853 were freed convict women. There were 630 farmers. In Van Diemen's Land there were 760 white people, and 700 on Norfolk Island. There were about 20 000 sheep, 20 000 pigs and 3500 goats.

Exploring New Holland

November 1804

Naturalist George Caley spends three weeks trying to cross the Blue Mountains.

He comes up against impenetrable cliff faces...

...and returns to Sydney defeated.

MAIDS, COOKS AND CROOKS

According to Governor King, the women of New South Wales were so wicked that neither kindness nor punishment could change them! Most of them were experienced criminals. Even the women who had followed their convict husbands to New South Wales had often helped their husbands to steal. The New South Wales Government supported 434 children as orphans because their mothers couldn't (or wouldn't) care for them.

'ello 'andsome.

In the early days, anyone who wanted to hire convict women chose them straight off the convict ship. The officers of the Rum Corps got first pick, then the enlisted men, then free settlers. Emancipists got the leftovers. Any woman who wasn't chosen had to find shelter and a job for herself. Many of the women ended up as wives, but most had no choice but to accept whatever a man offered them. After 1804 all convict women were first sent to the Female Factory at Parramatta. Those who weren't chosen for other jobs spun thread and wove cloth.

Ex-convict women usually weren't given land grants. There was plenty of work for them, but the jobs were usually terrible. Maids, nannies and cooks might work seventeen-hour days. If they swore—or even if they lifted their hand to protect themselves from a slap—they would be sent off for a flogging.

William Bligh.

CHAPTER 15

GOVERNOR BLIGH GIVES IT A TRY!

Governor King kept trying to clamp down on the Rum Corps. He tried to outlaw the distilling of alcohol from grain, but this didn't stop the Rum Corps. In fact, the Rum Corps and their friends were still doing pretty much exactly as they pleased. As well as buying rum from visiting ships, many of them were illegally brewing up a mix of wheat and sugar, then using a still to evaporate the alcohol. This homemade 'hooch' was so strong that it could blind the people who drank it—and was even known to kill people!

The Corps, of course, took no notice of Governor King's new law.

Floods, Fights and Famine

The colony was in trouble again. Autumn 1806 bought more floods to the Hawkesbury and the colony's grain crop was almost wiped out. There was still widespread theft and other problems from ex-convicts, ongoing attacks by the Eora and Bidjigal, and not enough government stores to feed convict gangs.

Another Guv Bites the Dust

The Corps had managed to get rid of yet another enemy—because Governor King resigned in August 1806. He was disappointed, ill and exhausted from battling with the Rum Corps and the crooks of the colony. But he had achieved many things, and left the colony a far better place than he had found it. The colony now had sealing and whaling industries, and factories for making leather, blankets, beer, rope and canvas. A new type of free settler was arriving, too—prosperous landowners who were given thousands of hectares, convicts and free passage in return for investing their wealth in the colony.

I need convicts who can carry luggage—immediately!

Bligh Takes the Helm

The new governor was Captain William Bligh. He had firm orders to impose order on the colony, and to stop the trade in alcohol by the Rum Corps. Bligh was determined, energetic and a sworn enemy of illegal activity. He was also tactless, and given to fits of swearing and rage. And he had very strong ideas about his right to rule. Surely a tough man like Bligh would be able to control the Rum Corps?

When Bligh was captain of the *Bounty* in 1789, his crew mutinied because of his harsh discipline. They cast him and a few loyal sailors adrift in a small boat, then sailed off to Pitcairn Island and founded a colony of mutineers.

Bligh Talks Tough!

To the delight of the free settlers, Bligh promised to crack down on the Rum Corps' activities. He declared that rum could no longer be used as money, and he increased the punishments for making illegal alcohol. Bligh also wasn't scared of punishing corrupt officials—or of offending anyone with his harsh temper. He sacked the Assistant Surgeon for stealing convicts from the hospital to work his own farm. And he closed the local paper when its editor published articles supporting the Rum Corps.

Macarthur Ignores the Law

John Macarthur had returned from England in 1805. He had never been court-martialled (due to the evidence against him 'disappearing'), so he was still a free man. And he hadn't changed a bit. Since returning, he had imported more illegal stills to make alcohol; he'd fenced in land that wasn't his; and he still demanded that people pay him in goods instead of money. On top of all that, he started a campaign against Governor Bligh.

Bligh put Macarthur on trial, charged with spreading rebellious ideas against the government. But during the trial the officers of the Rum Corps refused to obey Bligh's orders. Bligh ordered that Macarthur be jailed, but Major Johnston signed an order for Macarthur's release.

The squabble between the Rum Corps and the government was now an open battle. The Irish rebels had failed. But it looked like the rebellion of the English Rum Corps would succeed.

The Rum Rebellion

On 26 January 1808 John Macarthur and an unwilling Major Johnston led several hundred members of the New South Wales Corps in a march on Government House. Their bayonets were fixed ready to charge, fife and drum band played merrily, and most of them were drunk.

...you do the hokey pokey and you turn yourself around...

Bligh Beneath the Bed

Governor Bligh's widowed daughter, Mary Putland, bravely tried to defend the house. She dared the rebels to stab her to the heart, but to leave her father alone. Upstairs, Governor Bligh hid under a bed in a servant's bedroom. Bligh wasn't hiding because he was scared—his plan was to escape to the Hawkesbury, where he would raise an army of free settlers to fight the Corps.

But Bligh was discovered and dragged out from under the bed. Major Johnston declared that the Rum Corps now had complete control of the colony, and that he himself was in charge.

Caught me looking for a lost sock.

To celebrate this victory, the soldiers were served large amounts of alcohol and bonfires blazed across Sydney, with parties of drunks singing and yelling through the streets.

John Macarthur was declared innocent of all the charges against him and given a position of power.

Rounding up the Rebels

Major Johnston (but really Macarthur and the Rum Corps) had complete control of the colony for almost six months. In July Lieutenant-Colonel Joseph Foveaux arrived on his way to take control of Norfolk Island. He found New South Wales in complete turmoil. Foveaux had a higher rank than Major Johnston, so he took control away from Johnston and Macarthur, and then waited for instructions from England. But in those days it could be a year, or even two, before news arrived. In the meantime anything might happen.

Macarthur Duels Again!

Before Foveaux arrived, it was really Macarthur who was in charge of the colony. Macarthur was so angry with Foveaux that he challenged him to duel.

The men tossed a coin to see who would fire his pistol first. Macarthur won, fired—and missed! Foveaux refused to fire back. If he'd fired, he might have killed Macarthur, but Foveaux said there was no reason for the duel, and he hoped that by sparing Macarthur he would calm Macarthur's anger.

Try-Hard Bligh

Bligh was kept under house arrest, and wasn't allowed to leave Government House. But he kept trying to get support from the free settlers, who said that Bligh had just been trying to protect the colony. Foveaux refused to give Bligh back his job as governor. Bligh's actions may have been welcomed by many, but he had led the colony to disaster. Foveaux wanted Bligh to go back to England at once, before he could cause any more trouble.

Foveaux called Lieutenant-Governor Paterson back from Van Diemen's land, and Paterson reluctantly took over as governor. But Bligh continued to be a troublemaker. He went against Paterson's orders right up to the last minute. In

George
Johnston

William
Paterson

March 1809, as Bligh was about to sail back to England, he even tried to get the captain of the ship to arrest Paterson. The plan failed, and Paterson had Bligh arrested and taken to the barracks where he couldn't make a nuisance of himself.

Bligh finally left the colony a few days later, supposedly bound for England. But he took command of the ship and went to Hobart instead, and once again tried to drum up support. Lieutenant-Governor Collins had no choice but to forbid anyone to have anything to do with Bligh. Bligh's last effort to regain power had failed.

THE CROOKED CORPS RECALLED

The British Government finally recalled the Rum Corps to England. It was obvious that the Corps was totally out of control, and that no governor could run New South Wales while the Corps was around. The Corps was replaced by the 73rd Regiment, which had just finished serving in India, and it was commanded by Colonel Lachlan Macquarie.

Macquarie was appointed the new governor in May 1809. He arrived in Sydney in December. The leaders of the Rum Rebellion were charged with mutiny, while Bligh was forgiven for his behaviour and went on to become a vice-admiral.

Major George Johnston was drummed out of the army, but he was allowed to stay on his farm. The court believed his argument that he was an innocent man who had been mostly trying to restore order after a rebellion that Macarthur had organised! Macarthur escaped arrest by heading back into exile in England for another eight years.

Bligh died a few years later. He was bitter and disappointed, and he had been worn out by the trials of his governorship— just like Governors Phillip, Hunter and King had been before him.

THE LOVELY CONVICT LASS

Esther Abrahams was fifteen, and married, when she was sentenced to seven years for stealing two pieces of black lace in 1786.

Esther and her baby, Rosanna, came to Australia on the First Fleet aboard the *Lady Penrhyn*. Esther was beautiful and softly spoken, with long dark hair. She attracted the young officer, Lieutenant George Johnston, who had the job of keeping discipline on the ship. After their arrival in the colony they lived together, although they didn't marry—despite the fact that convict women who married free men were automatically freed. When George was posted to Norfolk Island, Esther went with him. She was treated as his wife, and not as a convict.

When George's period of service was up, he joined the New South Wales Corps rather than return to England and leave Esther behind. The two of them cleared their forty-hectare land grant in

Sydney and called it *Annandale*. Their homestead had its own butchery, bakery, blacksmith's forge, general store, orange orchard and vineyard. The driveway was lined with pines brought back as seedlings from Norfolk Island.

Esther and George became one of the wealthiest couples in New South Wales, with more land grants on the Georges River. Esther also received two large grants in her own name.

When George Johnston took control of the colony after the Rum Rebellion he moved into Government House, but Esther stayed behind and ran the farms. While George was away in England for four years being court-martialled for his role in the Rum Rebellion, Esther turned *Annandale* into one of the colony's best beef and horse studs.

In 1810 Governor Macquarie took away Esther's land grants because he disapproved of people living together without marrying, but three years later he met Esther in person and liked her so much that he gave her back the land.

George and Esther married in 1814. Had her first husband died? No-one will ever know. George's diaries mysteriously disappeared in the 1930s, possibly so that no-one would find out about the family's convict ancestor.

This will never make it into a history book.

Governor
Lachlan
Macquarie.

CHAPTER 16

A POOR FARMER'S LAD

Governor Lachlan Macquarie was the son of a poor Scottish farmer. He had neither family nor money behind him, and he had worked hard to earn his promotions. Macquarie's job was to improve the behaviour of the colonists; encourage marriage, farming and education; make alcohol illegal; and try to make the colony self-supporting so that it would no longer cost the British Government so much money.

Governor Macquarie had a great advantage over previous governors—his men were his own regiment and they would give him the loyalty and respect that none of the earlier governors who had to rely on the Rum Corps ever had.

Macquarie's Convict Mates

But Macquarie also made enemies. His first was the Reverend Samuel Marsden. Marsden was passionately anti-Catholic. He believed that the colony would be doomed within a year if Catholicism was ever made legal. Marsden also hated convicts. Macquarie, on the other hand, believed that once convicts had served their sentence, they should be treated like any other decent member of society. Over the years, he put many ex-convicts into positions of power and prestige—which some people didn't like at all.

By this time there were more emancipists in the colony than there were free settlers. Macquarie didn't want a colony where a small upper-class of free settlers had all the power while an underclass of ex-convicts had little or none.

> Wealthy British families often sent their unruly sons—or 'black sheep'—out to New South Wales to get them out of the way. Macquarie complained more about these young men than he ever did about convicts.

Grand Plans and Pricey Projects

Macquarie had grand plans for Sydney Town. He started the Bank of New South Wales and organised for a hospital to be built. He established a police service and a police court, had numbers placed on every house, and started an animal pound for stray animals, but these plans were expensive.

...and so that's how I came to be looking after you mutts.

Meanwhile, the ongoing Hawkesbury floods meant that the farmers only needed one convict out of every eight that were available. What was to be done with all the spare convicts?

Macquarie had a solution: he put them to work on his projects. But this meant that, instead of the farmers paying for the convicts' food, the government now had to pay. Since the crops had failed, this food had to be imported. And Macquarie's new buildings weren't cheap, even though they were built with convict labour.

So how much was the British Government prepared to spend on this colony at the end of the earth? The colony was too expensive. The British Government demanded to know why the colony had cost only £13 873 in 1806, but £72 000 in 1810. Macquarie explained that it couldn't be helped, but by 1814 the cost had ballooned to £100 000 a year—and it kept rising...

HOLEY DOLLAR!

In November 1811 Governor Macquarie bought £10 000 worth of Spanish dollars and had the middles stamped out of them. The *holey dollar* was worth five shillings, and the *dump* from the middle worth fifteen pence. Finally people had real money to spend, instead of paying with wheat or rum.

A Stroppy Lady

Mary Haydock ran away from the house where she was in service at the age of thirteen, disguised as a boy. She was caught trying to sell a stolen horse, and sentenced to seven years transportation in 1791. In 1794, while she was still a convict, she married the free settler and businessman Thomas Reibey.

Thomas and his business partner died in 1811, leaving Mary to cope with seven children and the property, as well as trading, shipping and sealing businesses in Sydney and Van Diemen's Land. With extraordinary energy and intelligence Mary expanded the many businesses, raised her family, became extremely rich and was active in many charitable works. Her portrait is on the twenty dollar note.

Piercing the Sandstone Curtain

For nearly a quarter of a century, the settlements of New South Wales had been walled in by the tall peaks and sheer cliffs of the Blue Mountains. What lay beyond?

BLAXLAND, WENTWORTH AND LAWSON

Gregory Blaxland was a farmer who wanted to find more grazing land for his cattle. William Lawson was a soldier and surveyor. William Charles Wentworth was the illegitimate son of a convict woman and a Second Fleet surgeon. His father had been arrested and tried for highway robbery four times, but was never convicted. William Wentworth later became a lawyer and vigorously defended ex-convicts; he founded a newspaper; and he took part in the last legal duel ever fought in the colony, over a quarrel with the governor.

Many white explorers had already failed to find a way across the Blue Mountains. In 1813 Blaxland, Lawson and Wentworth, along with four convicts, tried taking a different route. Instead of following creeks and rivers that ended in waterfalls; or trying to scale the cliffs in and out of the valleys, these three explorers followed the ridges. Perhaps they were following the example the Dharuk, who had been crossing the Blue Mountains for thousands of years.

It was a slow and dangerous expedition. There was little water or food for their horses, and the bush was often so thick they had to hack their way through. But after three weeks they finally looked down off the western escarpment.

A Path to the Plains

In 1814 Governor Macquarie sent artist and surveyor George Evans to explore the mountains and the land beyond. Evans reported that the country was superb. As well as excellent grassland, there were many rivers and streams; and the soil was fertile enough to feed the colony's sheep and cattle for more than a hundred years.

William Cox, a Hawkesbury magistrate and builder, got the job of building the first road through the mountains. He and his team of thirty finished 160 kilometres of road—with bridges and post-and-rail fences on the most dangerous sections—in the almost miraculous time of six months. As a reward for their hard work, the convicts were given their freedom.

Plains Passes Please!

In May 1815 Governor Macquarie headed west along the new road. His destination was the site of a new town on the Macquarie River. This town was going to be called Bathurst, after Lord Bathurst, the Colonial Secretary. Perhaps Macquarie hoped that if Lord Bathurst had a town named after him, he would stop complaining about the expense of the colony!

However, despite the lush feed—and the plentiful emus, kangaroos, cod fish, black swans, quail, pigeons and wild turkeys—Macquarie wasn't keen to let too many settlers cross the mountains. They'd be too far away from the watchful eye of the government, and who knows what they'd get up to? People had to get a pass to cross the mountains to the plains beyond. It wasn't until 1820 that Macquarie allowed settlers to graze their herds on the inland plains. Even then, it was only meant to be a temporary solution to a long drought, and the settlers weren't allowed to own the land their cattle grazed on.

By 1820 there were only about one hundred Europeans living west of the Blue Mountains, with about 30 000 sheep and cattle. Four years later there would be twelve hundred settlers, with more than 100 000 sheep and cattle.

TALKING FLASH

Convicts and emancipists had their own slang. *To speak good flash* meant to be able to use convict slang

Buzz: to pick a pocket.

Buzz cove: a pickpocket.

Chum: someone in jail. A *new chum* was in jail for a short time; an *old chum* for a long time.

Eating a Norfolk dumpling: getting 100 lashes.

Doing the Norfolk hornpipe: a hanged man twitching on the gallows.

But I can't dance!

Thomas Davey

CHAPTER 17

WILD COLONIAL BOYS

Meanwhile, the colony in Van Diemen's Land was growing, but trouble was brewing, too. From 1807 onwards the Norfolk Island convicts and free settlers started arriving, boosting the numbers in the tiny settlement. Governor Macquarie visited in 1811 to check on progress (he thought Hobart was too messy, and ordered a proper plan); and the first shipment of new convicts arrived on 19 October 1812, with 199 convicts. Amongst these convicts was Michael Howe. He was an army and navy deserter and would soon become the colony's most feared bushranger. Another 125 women convicts arrived soon afterwards.

'MAD TOM' DAVEY

Accompanying the female convicts was the new governor of Van Diemen's Land, Thomas Davey. He had once been accused of stealing money when he was paymaster for the First Fleet marines so, although he was now the governor, he wasn't allowed anywhere near public money.

Macquarie thought Davey was a buffoon and a drunk. Davey thought Macquarie was a prig. Macquarie wouldn't let Davey do anything without getting Macquarie's permission first. Davey said Macquarie made it almost impossible for Davey to do his job.

Both men had a point.

> Some of the fire-hollowed trees in Van Diemen's Land were so enormous that whole families were able to live in them while they built their huts.

THE BUSHRANGER WARS

The worst criminals and most dangerous convicts were sent to Van Diemen's Land, usually as a punishment for having committed crimes while still serving sentences in New South Wales. Far more convicts arrived than this tiny colony could look after.

There were many convicts at large in the bush, still there after escaping with their muskets while hunting for meat in the colony's early years. Now more escaped convicts started joining them, as well as sailors who had deserted their ships. These bushrangers 'ranged' across the colony, terrorising settlers, stealing food and stock and even taking over farmhouses. Some settlers moved back to the safety of the towns. Others just did what the bushrangers told them to.

In 1814 a desperate Governor Macquarie offered an amnesty to all bushrangers. If they returned to their jobs, they would be pardoned—providing they hadn't committed murder. A few bushrangers surrendered, but most ignored the offer.

Then a reward of fifty guineas was offered to anyone who could provide information about a bushranger. However, this was risky! John Whitehead, the leader of the biggest gang, filled 'Looney' Hopkins' moccasins with bull ants as punishment for giving evidence against the bushrangers. The shoes were tied to Hopkins' feet and he died in agony. Hardly anyone dared to dob in a bushranger!

Governor Davey sent soldiers out into the hills to find the bushrangers' hideouts. But there were too few soldiers—and too much wild country for the bushrangers to hide in. Finally, without Macquarie's permission, Davey declared that any person who was caught committing murder, robbery or rape would be court-martialled and executed. But even this wasn't enough to stop the bushrangers.

DAVEY GETS DUMPED

'Mad Tom' Davey soon became a laughing stock. He poured port over his wife's hat; ladled out free rum to passers-by; didn't bother to keep records; and wandered about the streets without his coat on. This was *not* what gentlemen did! By 1816 his behaviour became too much for Macquarie, who gave Davey the chance to resign with a large grant of land. If Davey didn't accept, he would be embarrassingly sacked. Davey accepted, and Colonel William Sorell took over as governor.

THE CONVICT ARMY OF MICHAEL HOWE

For a while the most feared bushranger in Van Diemen's Land was Michael Howe. The 'last and worst' of the bushrangers arrived when he was twenty-four. He had been convicted of highway robbery in England, then charged with violence again in New South Wales before being sent to Van Diemen's Land. After repeated floggings for further violence, he quickly absconded.

By 1814 he and a fellow escaped convict named Whitehead had gathered a gang of twenty-eight bushrangers and moulded them into a disciplined convict rebel army. Howe had in fact helped many of these convicts to escape. When Whitehead died, Howe took over as leader of the gang. He kept the men under military discipline, and each member had to swear an oath of loyalty.

Almost two people out of every hundred in Van Diemen's Land ended up in Howe's army!

Howe was a natural leader, a giant of a man with a long beard who dressed in kangaroo skins. He had enormous energy and a gift for organisation. His gang of bushrangers raided farms right across the island, from Hobart to Port Dalrymple. They also raided Aboriginal camps to capture women for themselves.

Best simply to avoid trouble.

Howe!

Avoid Howe.

Howe captured an Aboriginal woman, Mary, to be his wife. Despite this savage beginning, Howe and Mary grew very close. It was Mary who helped him outwit the military groups that were regularly sent to capture him. Then Mary, pregnant with Howe's child, was shot by a white soldier. Howe abandoned her. Perhaps he thought she was dead or dying— but Mary survived and, in revenge, offered to help the authorities to track him down. They weren't successful. Howe grew more and more savage. He eventually broke with his gang and increasingly operated on his own.

Finally, in 1818, a kangaroo hunter and two companions found Howe camped under a gum tree near his hut by the Shannon River. A tremendous fight followed, with the three men pitted against the lone bushranger. By the time it was over Howe's brains had been bashed out. His body was buried by his hut, and his broken head removed and taken to Hobart where it was put on display as a deterrent to other would-be bushrangers.

HAIRCUTS 1p.

I don't care what it's up there for. It's scaring off customers.

Howe's captors found a diary in his hut. It listed all the flowers Howe had known back home in Yorkshire, and that he wanted to grow around his hut. The diary was written in Howe's blood—or someone's blood, at any rate!

William Sorell.

SORELL SORTS IT OUT

William Sorell was much more organised than Davey. He caught and hanged most of Howe's gang, sent troopers to keep the new farmlands safe from bushrangers, built convict barracks and generally cleaned up the mess that Davey had left. Sorell even coped with the huge numbers of convicts that kept arriving in Van Diemen's Land, partially by creating the most feared prison in the English-speaking world—the dreaded Macquarie Harbour.

Immigrants flowed into the new colony, and Van Diemen's Land became the whaling and sealing capital of the southern hemisphere. Farms spread quickly along the Derwent and Tamar Rivers, first growing wheat, and then breeding sheep for their wool. In 1820 the Van Diemen's Land Government bought nearly two hundred merino rams from the Macarthurs to improve the quality of wool. Sheep flourished on the grasslands of the midlands—and the descendants of these sheep would eventually give the finest wool in the world.

But the growing farm success led to more competition with the Aboriginal people for land and game. Within a few years this would lead to one of the world's great tragedies.

NAUGHTY SORELL GETS THE SACK

Sorell was very popular with the Van Diemen's Land colonists. In fact he was so popular that the free settlers gave him a dinner service of silver plate worth five hundred guineas. However, Sorell lived with another man's wife, even though he had a wife and seven children of his own at home in England. This caused gossip back in Britain, and the gossips finally ruined Sorell's reputation so badly that he was recalled in 1824. He was never given another job.

Bungaree

CHAPTER 18

MACQUARIE MARCHES ON

For the first time since Governor Phillip, New South Wales had a governor who was interested in the original people of the land. Phillip had been interested in how the Eora lived. But Macquarie wanted the Aboriginal people to give up their 'wandering predatory habits' and become farm labourers or skilled craftsmen. He hoped that 'kindness and encouragement' would inspire the Aboriginal people to follow British ways.

In 1815 he set up a school for Aboriginal children at Parramatta with six boys and six girls. They were to be taught reading, writing and arithmetic. The boys were to learn how to farm, and the girls how to be servants. But most of the children either left or were taken away by their parents, and even those who did brilliantly at school still preferred their own culture to the British. The school closed in 1823.

Macquarie also started a farm settlement scheme at Port Jackson, where sixteen carefully selected Aboriginal men, led by 'King' Bungaree, were given tools, clothes, huts and a boat for fishing. But the huts were broken up and the bark sold, and the project only lasted a few months.

VIOLENCE BREEDS VIOLENCE

Not many settlers shared Macquarie's views on the Aboriginal people. Even his Chief Judge, Ellis Bent, declared that they were incapable of civilisation. And as had been happening all along, attacks by one side led to retaliation by the other, leading to still further attacks. A shepherd was speared, his body mutilated and his two hundred sheep killed. Then five more settlers were killed.

In reprisal for these attacks, Macquarie sent a military party out to the Grose, Neapean and Hawkesbury farming areas in 1816. He ordered the soldiers to capture any Aboriginal person they found; and shoot anyone who resisted, and hang their bodies from the trees. Fourteen Bidjigal men, women and children were killed when troops broke into their encampment; five were captured; and others jumped from the cliffs rather than face the soldiers and their guns.

From then on, no Aboriginal person was allowed to carry a weapon near a white settlement, and no more than six Aboriginal people were allowed to gather together.

Parramatta Peace Party

Macquarie still wanted to make peace with the Aboriginals. So he announced that there would be a Congress of Friendly Natives every year on 28 December at Parramatta, which was the traditional meeting place of the Bidjigal people.

The first such congress in 1816 was attended by 179 Aboriginal people. They feasted on roast beef, potatoes, bread, and a cask of rum. Macquarie gave badges of distinction to the 'chiefs' and badges of merit to anyone who had helped soldiers track down outlawed Aboriginal men.

A sad sort of peace had finally been reached in the Sydney area. The traditional landowners were now outnumbered by the new settlers. Many had been killed by disease, by weapons and by alcohol. Their traditional country had been turned into farms, which meant they had to beg for food, or else live on minimum wages or basic rations, working on farms that had once been their land.

BUNGAREE OF THE GURINGAI PEOPLE

Bungaree was well-known around the settlements for his skills as a seafarer and fisherman, as well as for his politeness and general good humour. He was a good middleman when there were disputes between the British and Aboriginal people, and helped the Aboriginal people understand the British customs.

Bungaree accompanied Flinders on his two 1799 explorations, and again on his 1801–02 circumnavigation of New Holland. He also went with Phillip Parker King on his explorations of north-west Australia in 1816–17.

Governor Macquarie gave Bungaree a name plate which said *Bungaree, Chief of the Broken Bay Tribe, 1815*, and put him in charge of a farm. When the farm failed, Macquarie gave Bungaree a boat and net for commercial fishing.

Like Bennelong, Bungaree was eventually overwhelmed by the difficult balancing act of being the go-between for two such different cultures. By 1826 Bungaree was a clownish figure in a plumed hat and a British jacket wearing a brass plate that proclaimed him *Bungaree, King of Sydney Cove*. He died an alcoholic in 1830.

Corpse and Robber Ships

Life on board convict ships was still appalling. Convicts wore heavy shackles sometimes weighing seven kilograms or more. Their possessions and food rations were stolen by stewards, cooks, overseers and captains.

Ships' doctors even 'helped' sick convicts to die in order to sell their bodies. The only way you could improve your lot was by bribing someone. About one in every thirty convicts died on the voyage.

In 1814 typhus killed so many convicts and crew on the *Surrey* that a crew from another ship had to bring it to shore. Horrified at this death ship, the colony's assistant surgeon at the time, William Redfern, who was himself an ex-convict, suggested that there should be a minimum standard of living for the convicts. This should include warm clothing and daily visits to the deck for fresh air.

He also recommended that captains should no longer be allowed to sell the food, medicines or clothing that had been supplied by the British Government for the convicts.

The new rules made a great difference. The death rate plummeted, though life on board a convict ship would never be pleasant—the ships were crowded and stinking, and prisoners were chained to each other. And now that the war with France was over, Britain had spare ships to be filled with convicts. In 1814 more than one thousand convicts arrived, and more and more arrived each year.

WATER WORRIES

Living conditions in the colony were still basic. The only way of getting water was to lug it in buckets from a creek which might be a couple of kilometres away. There were no hoses, no galvanised iron water tanks—and not even any tin roofs to catch the rainwater. Most houses had water barrels. It was the children's job to fill these with buckets of water they'd carried from the creek. When people got to the bottom of the barrel they would have to scoop out the dead mosquitoes, spiders, cockroaches and millipedes that had fallen in during the week.

GREEN LIGHT FOR GREENWAY

Macquarie was making more enemies because he kept giving emancipists jobs as solicitors and magistrates. A particularly unpopular move was to give an emancipist the job of government architect in 1816. Francis Greenway had been transported for forgery, but now he was to be paid three shillings a day, be provided with quarters for himself and his family, as well as a horse and food for the horse. Macquarie asked Greenway to draw up plans for churches at Sydney, Windsor and Liverpool; a lighthouse at South Head; and a new factory and barracks for the convict women at Parramatta.

Harsher Rules Rule

Macquarie also had Greenway design a new three-storey convict barracks which could house about eight hundred men—or a third of Sydney's convicts. The remaining convicts either lived with their employers or—if they were married and well-behaved—with their wives and families. After 1816 they worked for food instead of wages, and were given clean clothes twice a week, marked with arrows and their barrack number. Well-behaved convicts were allowed out at weekends. It was a stricter system—and it worked. Once the worst of the convicts were locked up for the night, there was only one tenth the amount of crime in Sydney.

The name *Australia* was becoming popular in the colony. *New Holland* only referred to the part that had been claimed by the Dutch. In 1817 Macquarie recommended that *Australia* become official.

Avagood weekend.

Exploring Australia

The Voyage of the Mermaid 1817–1818

THE HUNT FOR THE INLAND SEA CONTINUES...

Lieutenant Phillip Parker King was the son of former Governor King.

He was commissioned to see if there was a river that led inland from the northern coast of the continent.

Sea?

He sailed in the Mermaid.

He discovered plagues of flies,

turtles

seasnakes,

hot winds and barren country.

But no great river.

Finally, at the northern coast, King came across great grasslands.

And the first good harbour which he named...

Port Essington

But provisions were running low and the ship and water casks were leaking.

'clop'

So King Jr returned to Sydney...

Then in 1817 the Surveyor-General, John Oxley, took two portable boats down the Lachlan River to continue the search.

The Lachlan River vanished into swamps

Croak.

and lagoons with poor soil and stunted trees.

The Macquarie River led Oxley to better land with richer soil and larger trees.

But there was still no inland sea.

Squawk!

CHAPTER 19

MONEY TALKS, MACQUARIE WALKS

By 1817 Macquarie was exhausted. He was tired of battling for the rights of ex-convicts, and the British Government kept moaning about the cost of his building campaigns. So Macquarie offered his resignation. However, his letter had to travel by ship to England, and the reply had to come back the same way. While he waited, Macquarie soldiered on.

Sydney was now a sizeable town. It boasted the grand public buildings Macquarie had so wanted. As well as St James Church, the hospital, the lighthouse and the convict barracks, there were proper roads and big solid houses with gardens, orchards and parks. About 25 000 white settlers, soldiers and convicts now lived in New South Wales.

There was a new whaling station at Twofold Bay (now Eden). The wool of the merino sheep was getting high prices from English woollen mills. A new toll road linked Parramatta with Emu Ford on the Nepean River. The road over the Blue Mountains had opened up the pastoral lands on the Macquarie River, and settlers were farming the rich lands of the Hunter Valley and the Bathurst Plains.

> The export of fine merino wool turned Australia from a dumping ground for convicts into an exciting land for pioneers.

MACQUARIE GOES FOR BROKE

Back in Britain the Colonial Office was still asking questions. The colony cost more and more each year! Convict labour was building a new nation on the other side of the world—but was it worthwhile sending convicts so far? Was the punishment of convicts in New South Wales harsh enough to scare would-be wrongdoers in England? Was the colony getting too big? Should Australia be known as a land of opportunity for free settlers—or as a place of fear and shame for convicts?

Many members of the British Government just wanted a harsh and cheap penal colony. In 1819 they sent Mr John Thomas Bigge, a lawyer, to investigate the colony, and to write a report on what he saw. The suggestions in this report were to be obeyed at once by the government of the colony.

It was an insult to Governor Macquarie that when Bigge was in Sydney, he chose to stay with the notorious John Macarthur, whose opinions matched his own.

Meanwhile Macquarie struggled to find work, food and housing for the growing number of convicts. With the Napoleonic Wars in Europe over, soldiers (many of them wounded and unable to work) turned to crime just to put bread in their mouths. And more crime in England meant more convicts for New South Wales—and even more cost to feed them. Many convicts were sent straight to Van Diemen's Land. The worst criminals worked on the roads in chain gangs. Macquarie set up a government farm at Emu Plains just to create work for the overflow of convicts.

THE BEST CON FOR THE JOB

When a convict ship arrived, the government got first pick of the convicts. Convicts who had been builders, bricklayers or masons were badly needed on building projects. But the convicts knew that they would have an easier time if they worked for free settlers, so many of them lied about their skills. New settlers got second pick so they could start working their farms. Wealthy farmers often started farms in the names of their family and servants so they could get an extra lot of convicts assigned to them. But only one convict in five had ever worked on a farm before coming to Australia. Even if they turned out to be unskilled or lazy, the free settlers weren't allowed to give them back. The leftover convicts did things like digging drains.

HOW MANY CONVICTS STAYED IN AUSTRALIA?

There are no accurate records. Many convicts died on the voyage out, or soon after they arrived. Of 122 Irish convicts who landed in Australia in 1791, only fifty were alive a year later. Many convicts returned to Britain once they'd served their sentence, or left for the South Seas or America. Perhaps thirty percent stayed—and survived. But these figures are mostly guesswork.

BIGGE CLASH WITH MACQUARIE

Bigge and Macquarie squabbled almost at once. Macquarie wanted to appoint ex-convict William Redfern as a magistrate. Bigge declared that it was not a suitable position for an ex-convict. Colonial Secretary Lord Bathurst backed Bigge.

Macquarie plugged on. He continued his work, establishing the New South Wales Savings Bank to look after 'the savings of the industrious poor'. To the horror of some people, a number of the bank directors were emancipists. He laid down traffic rules—all carts, horses and cattle had to keep to the left side of the road.

He also put forward the idea of setting up Aboriginal reserves, away from white settlements, where the Aboriginal people might be taught how to take up the European way of life. It was a well-intentioned idea by a good-hearted man, but it was to have tragic consequences.

However, everyone—including Macquarie himself — knew that his time as governor was coming to an end. The colony waited for Bigge's report, and for the decisions of the British Government about the colony's future.

LAND OF HOPE AND WORRY

By 1820 the struggling convict colony had become Australia. It had towns from Hobart to Newcastle, farms from the Hunter Valley to Bathurst and Mudgee; cattle as far south as the Limestone Plains (Canberra) and Twofold Bay on the south coast. Sydney was a growing city instead of a collection of wattle-and-daub huts.

Australia's shores were mapped. Ships sailed to and from Europe, the Americas, China and India. There were seemingly endless grasslands, whales, seals, timbers, rivers and game. And beyond the existing settlements there seemed to be land and a future for anyone who wished to claim it.

Unless you were Aboriginal. For them, things were going downhill. Though they still controlled more than ninety percent of the continent, European settlement and introduced illnesses were taking a heavy toll.

Though the British had mapped the coastline, they had explored very little of the interior. Was there a great sea? Or a vast civilisation hidden by mountain ranges?

Much of the colony's prosperity was based on free convict labour. But although Australia had a wealth of land, it was a long way from countries that might buy its wool and other produce.

For the time being, however, things looked good. But if the British decided that the colony was too expensive, or if they found cheaper solutions for the convict problem and sent them somewhere else, would the colony in Australia survive?

Making Sense of Shillings and Cents

When the British came to Australia they used the *sterling* system of money: pounds, shillings and pence. There were twelve pennies (pence) in one shilling, and twenty shillings in one pound; a guinea was worth one pound, one shilling—very complicated.

Australia used this system until 1966, when it adopted the *decimal* system: dollars and cents. It's much easier—all you have to know is how to divide and multiply by ten. Since 1971 the British have also been using the decimal system, but now there are one hundred pennies in a pound, and there are no shillings or guineas.

In *Grim Crims & Convicts* we have left all amounts of money in the old pounds, shillings and pence that were used at the time. There is really no way of properly converting amounts from the historical sterling to modern decimal currency.

Records tell us that the average wage in England in the late 1700s was five shillings a week. As you can see on page 130, five shillings couldn't buy you very much in Sydney at the time!

INDEX